Dedication

During the writing of this book my mother, Mary Sweitzer, went home to be with the Lord. What a great influence she had upon my life! She lived 90 years—74 as a born-again Christian, and a half century as a Spirit-filled believer. Mother was the first to instruct me in God's grace, and she did it in the most convincing manner possible: she lived it. I lovingly dedicate this book about grace to a woman who is now enjoying the ultimate reward of grace—my dear mother, Mary Sweitzer.

You Can!
Bounce Back
From Your
Setback

The 5 Best Ways

by Marilyn Hickey

**Marilyn
Hickey
Ministries**
P.O. Box 17340
Denver, CO 80217

You Can!
Bounce Back
From Your
Setback

The 5 Best Ways

Copyright © 1999 by Marilyn Hickey Ministries
P.O. Box 17340
Denver, Colorado 80217

ISBN 1-56441-040-4
Printed in the United States of America

Unless otherwise indicated, all Scripture quotations
are taken from the *King James Version* of the Bible.

TABLE OF CONTENTS

PREFACE

Most people live *far* beneath the level of blessing that is available for their lives because they feel *unworthy*. If you feel that you aren't good enough to be used and blessed by God, remember that...

Moses stuttered.
David was too small for his armor.
John Mark got homesick and quit his ministry.
Hosea's wife was a prostitute.
Amos' only training was in fig tree pruning.
Jacob was a liar and deceiver.
David had an affair.
Solomon was too rich.
Abraham was too old.
David was too young.
Jesus was too poor.
Timothy had ulcers.
Peter denied Jesus because of a young girl's
　　　ridicule.
Lazarus was dead.
John was self-righteous.
Naomi was a widow.
Moses, David, and Paul were murderers.
Jonah ran away from God.
Miriam was a gossip.
Gideon and Thomas both doubted.

Jeremiah was depressed and suicidal.
Elijah was burned out.
John the Baptist was a loudmouth.
Martha was a worrywart.
Samson's hair was too long.
Noah got drunk.
Moses, Peter, and Paul had temper problems.

I'm not suggesting that you take pride in your shortcomings or that you continue in them, but by *grace*—God can bless and use you *anyway*. As you grasp the truth of God's "System of Blessing," you will be freed to become... EVERYTHING GOD HAS CALLED YOU TO BE.

Chapter One

DON'T UNDERESTIMATE THE POWER OF GOD'S GRACE

DON'T UNDERESTIMATE THE POWER OF GOD'S GRACE

He that spared not his own Son, but delivered him up for us all, how shall he not with him also freely give us all things?
(Romans 8:32).

As I left my home for the airport, I thought, "No, God won't heal me. If I'm sick, it's my own fault."

I had booked myself too tightly and overtaxed my body. I felt like boarding my bed instead of the airplane that would take me to Moscow, Russia, and, after a brief layover, on to Novosibirsk, Siberia, for a week-long crusade and pastor's conference. The following week, I was scheduled for several days of meetings in Almaty, Kazakstan, and the week after that, I was to go to Riga, Latvia. I couldn't even blame the devil for my physical condition; it was my own fault. I'd been working too hard.

Just the week before, I had taken a group of nearly 300 people to minister at various ports on the East Coast of Africa. Then, I had held a week-long, citywide crusade in Tanga, Tanzania. Somewhere along the way, I became ill. Not only did I have a miserable cold that had kept me awake at night coughing, but I had somehow hurt my back, too! Now, I faced a flight of 20 hours over three days, and three very long, intense weeks of ministry.

As the airplane left the runway and began climbing to cruising altitude, I knew that I could not make it through the next three weeks without God's help. However, the truth was, after the way I had treated my body, I felt I didn't "deserve" to be healed. As the engines of the airplane droned, the enemy chanted over and over in my mind: "You deserve to be sick! You deserve to be sick."

After spending days in airplane seats, I finally arrived in Novosibirsk, Siberia. I was so sick and sore that I could hardly stand. I wondered, "What will people think when they see me hobbling to the platform to pray for the sick?"

Although I thought that I didn't deserve to be healed, I began to pray and believe God for His promise of healing. I didn't get what I "deserved," I got what I needed—God's grace. God healed me!

Getting what you need from God instead of what you deserve is what the Bible calls *grace*. Grace is the way God wants to relate to you and me. Too often, we miss out on His best because we feel unworthy to receive it.

Grace Is . . .

Many, many Christians miss out on God's best for their lives—not because of sin, or things they're doing or not doing, but because they do not understand and receive God's *grace*. Grace is not something *natural* that we can cause to happen but something *supernatural* that comes only from God. We can even receive His grace when we sin. Grace is everything you need to live the "abundant life" which is God's best for you. The abundant life is what Jesus purchased for you at great cost on the cross: *"...I am come that they might have life, and that they might have it more abundantly"* (John 10:10).

GRACE

Favor or kindness shown without regard to the worth or merit of the one who receives it, and in spite of what that same person deserves. Grace is one of the key attributes of God. The Lord God is *"merciful and gracious, long-suffering, and abounding in goodness and truth"* (Exodus 34:6 NKJ). Therefore, grace is almost always associated with mercy, love, compassion, and patience as the source of help and with deliverance from distress.

(Used by permission from *Nelson's Illustrated Bible Dictionary.* Copyright © 1986, Thomas Nelson Publishers)

Grace is the beginning and end of what God has done, is doing, and will do for you. In fact, grace is the story of God's relationship with mankind. God's grace, His *unearned* favor, is possibly the most misunderstood teaching in our day. Nevertheless, it is unquestionably one of the most important. *Grace is getting more than we expect and less than we deserve from the One who loves us.*

The basis for grace is love–God's great love for you and me as individuals:

> But God demonstrates His own love toward
> us, in that while we were still sinners, Christ
> died for us (Romans 5:8 NKJ).

Unfortunately, for many Christians, God's grace begins and ends with salvation. Few question that salvation is through grace: "...*by grace you have been saved through faith,...*" (Ephesians 2:8 NKJ). Nor is there any doubt that salvation is the highest achievement of grace. What we have misunderstood is that salvation is merely the entrance to the wonderful garden of grace that God has prepared for us. To become all that God wants us to be, we need to understand God's system of blessing called *grace*.

Is God Fair? (God's System of Blessing)

> ...*they complained against the landowner*
> [God], *saying, 'These last men have worked*
> *only one hour, and you made them equal to*
> *us who have borne the burden and the heat of*
> *the day'* (Matthew 20:11,12 NKJ).

Because I read through the Bible every year, eventually, I come across the parable told by Jesus in Matthew 20:1-15; but until recently, I haven't fully understood what God was trying to say. Now I have the key to this parable—the secret to understanding it is "grace."

The parable tells the story of a landowner, symbolizing God, who hired day laborers to gather his grape harvest. He hired some of the men early in the morning, and told them he would pay them a specific wage, a denarius; he hired others throughout the day and told them he would pay them "whatever is right." (Some of the men worked all day and others as little as one hour.) When the vineyard owner paid everyone the same, a denarius, the ugly scene in Matthew 20:11,12 occurred.

We know that God is scrupulously fair, perfectly honest, and unfailingly impartial. However, it didn't seem fair to give the laborers who worked all day long the same pay as those who worked only one hour. The one-hour workers would make *12 times more* than those who had worked hard the whole day! For a long time, I could not understand how that could be "fair."

The clue to understanding is found in the first five words of the parable, *"For the kingdom of heaven..."* (Matthew 20:1). In other words, this is not a labor union situation. This story does not even occur in our world. This parable illustrates how the kingdom of heaven—and therefore, God—operates.

First, God tells us that He doesn't hire according to *His* need; He hires according to *our* need. We must face the fact that God can get along just fine and successfully achieve what He wants to accomplish on this earth *without us*. If you or I disappeared, He could find someone to do what we do, and possibly do it even better. We need to let go of any ego trip we are on about how badly God *needs* us and realize that we are the ones who need the job He has given to us.

Second, God's payroll policy isn't based upon the union wage scale or "comparable wages" within our industry. Instead, God pays us what we need. The daily wage in Jesus' day was one denarius. That was the amount a person needed each day to live. It did not matter whether a person worked 12 hours or one hour a day; they still needed a denarius each day to live. Since God pays what we need rather than what we earn, from God's point of view it made perfect sense to pay each man a denarius, regardless of how long he had worked.

Perhaps you are thinking that you happen to need a lot of things, and wonder why God's grace isn't operating very powerfully in your life. Just as some people fail to grasp their opportunity for salvation, many Christians fail to get hold of the "abundance" provisions of God's grace.

In the following pages, we will look at some of the reasons why people miss God's best for their lives. Perhaps you will see yourself in some of these scenarios. The "rich young ruler" was one such person; He really missed out on a huge opportunity to enjoy God's grace.

10,000% Increase

And every one that hath forsaken houses, or brethren, or sisters, or father, or mother, or wife, or children, or lands, for my name's sake, shall receive an hundredfold, and shall inherit everlasting life. But many that are first shall be last; and the last shall be first (Matthew 19:29).

The story of a young man who missed a 10,000 percent increase is found in Matthew 19:16-22. On one occasion a wealthy young man came to Jesus and asked, *"...what good thing shall I do, that I may have eternal life?"* (Matthew 19:16). Jesus asked him a series of questions about whether he had kept the Jewish law. To every question the young man answered, "Yes."

Then Jesus said something extremely important:

> ... *If thou wilt be perfect* [which means mature], *go and sell that thou hast, and give to the poor, and thou shalt have treasure in heaven: and come and follow me. But when the young man heard that saying, he went away sorrowful: for he had great possessions* (Matthew 19:21,22).

God does not expect us to be perfect but He does want us to become mature. When we develop in our understanding of our relationship with God, we release God's provisions of grace in our lives.

This young man wanted to earn grace by the merit system—doing "good things" to receive God's grace. Jesus challenged him to go beyond the merit system, to give everything away, and get on the "grace system." God is doing the same thing today; He is challenging you, not necessarily to give everything you own away, but to trade the merit system for grace.

Just eight verses later, Jesus explains the benefits of the grace system. As often happened at the end of the day, the disciples were questioning Jesus about things that had occurred during the day. The incident with the rich, young ruler must have been on their minds when Jesus said:

> *And everyone who has left houses or brothers or sisters or father or mother or children or fields for my sake will receive a hundred times as much and will inherit eternal life* (Matthew 19:29) NIV.

The rich young man not only missed out on eternal life and the incredible opportunity to become a disciple of Jesus, he missed becoming the wealthiest man in Israel. He could have received 10,000 times what he gave away—and the Bible says he was extremely wealthy! ("One hundred times" is 10,000 percent.) Being possessed by your possessions can cost you everything—just as it did the rich young ruler. However, by placing your relationship with God on the "merit system," you lose even more...the "abundant life."

The Merit System

> *...do not set aside the grace of God; for if righteousness comes through the law, then Christ died in vain* (Galatians 2:21 NKJ).

It is easy to put yourself on the merit system with God. It comes naturally because it is the system we know from childhood. If we are good, then we get a reward. If we work hard, then we get ahead in life. As a result, we think we have "earned" points with God when we go to church, pray, read the Bible, do good deeds, witness, pay tithes, give offerings, volunteer at church, and so on.

We have confused God's system of blessing with the world's system of reward and punishment. We feel the same way that the men who had worked all day in the vineyard felt: we "deserve" God's blessings because we have done so much for Him. Although we would never put it in these terms, we feel God is *obligated* to do well by us.

Please do not misunderstand, we *should* go to church, pray, read the Bible, give, and do all those things which are good and right. We should try to please God by the way we live, and we should expect a reward for doing the right thing. (Each godly action is as a seed sowed; it *will* bring a rightful reward.) However, we should not make the mistake of thinking we have somehow indebted God by our actions.

Have you ever thought or even prayed, "God, I've worked so hard for you. I pay my tithes. I volunteer at church. I do this and I do that. Why can't you just bless me a little more financially this month?" or "Why won't you heal me of this illness?"

> *Woe to the one who quarrels with his maker—*
> *an earthenware vessel among the vessels of*
> *earth! Will the clay say to the potter, 'What*
> *are you doing?'...* (Isaiah 45:9 NAS).

When I was sick during that flight to Russia, God did not heal me because I deserved healing or even because I needed healing. I had not obligated God to heal me because I was doing His work or had put in extra hours for the kingdom. No! No! No! God healed me for the same reason He heals you or anyone else—FAITH. I had faith in His Word that says Jesus bore my sickness, carried my diseases, and that by His stripes I am healed (see Isaiah 53:4,5). *It is not through merit, but through faith by grace that you will receive God's promises.*

Have you ever wondered why a dear saint in the church who has worked long and hard for the Lord dies of cancer, while a sinner walks into the church (out of years of sin and wrongdoing) and receives a miraculous healing? The reason one person receives and another does not is that one believes in God's *grace with faith* for His promise, while the other does not. Neither healing nor any of God's blessings are doled out because of merit; rather, they are brought into our lives by *faith.*

A few years after Wally and I were married, we decided we wanted a child. We tried for several years and nothing happened. The doctor said we couldn't have a child. Finally I got unhappy with God and said, "I'm serving you. I am in ministry. I work hard. I memorize Scripture. I should be pregnant!" Do you know what happened next? Nothing! Not a thing! Eventually, I got the message and prayed, "God, you know my desire to have a child but if You never want me to have one, that's wonderful. I leave this thing in Your hands." Guess what happened next? I became pregnant. The blessing came when I quit trying to receive from God through my *own* merit and just left it to His grace. To get into God's grace, we must surrender to it.

We actually frustrate God's grace when we get into the merit system with God because He will not allow us to put a price tag on that which He has freely given. When we declare our own merit to God, we are boasting that we have earned the right (self-righteousness) by our actions to receive from Him:

I do not frustrate the grace of God: for if righteousness come by the law, then Christ is dead in vain (Galatians 2:21).

Paul said about self-righteousness, *"...There is none righteous, no, not one:"* (Romans 3:10). We can never be "good enough" to merit the blessings of God; our *only* hope is in His grace. Throw away self-righteousness and the merit system, and throw yourself upon God's mercy. Then you will discover as Paul did...*"And he said unto me, My grace is sufficient for thee:..."* (II Corinthians 12:9).

The Demerit System

For I am persuaded, that neither death, nor life, nor angels, nor principalities, nor powers, nor things present, nor things to come, Nor height, nor depth, nor any other creature, shall be able to separate us from the love of God, which is in Christ Jesus our Lord (Romans 8:38,39).

Many Christians teeter-totter between trying to merit God's love and grace and feeling unworthy to receive it. The simple fact is—God's love and grace are free. Satan says to you, "You're not worthy" but Jesus answers for you, "But *I am* worthy and you are within me." Satan looks back and sees your mistakes, but God looks back and sees the cross! God does not remember what you did wrong in 1979 or '99. Your past mistakes are not even a part of God's record if you have confessed them. They are buried deep under the blood of Christ.

If we believe that we must be good enough to receive from God then we will also believe that we are bad enough to miss God's blessing. We say to ourselves, "I'm so unworthy. God would never heal me, prosper me, or use me." This attitude is self-reinforcing because our feelings of unworthiness undermine our faith and, without faith, it is impossible to receive from God. Then, when we do not receive, we whine, "I prayed and believed but nothing happened. I knew God would never do anything for the likes of me."

It is true; we can never be worthy of God's goodness. However, God found a way around that roadblock. Instead of making His blessings the wages of our good acts (the merit system), He put His priceless blessings beyond price by making them free (the grace system).

God's Grace vs. Sowing and Reaping

For no matter how many promises God has made, they are "Yes" in Christ. And so through him the "Amen" is spoken by us to the glory of God (II Corinthians 1:20 NIV).

No promise in the Bible is dependent upon your performance. This is too important a truth to say only once. Read this carefully, write it down and shout it with great joy! **NO PROMISE IS DEPENDENT UPON YOUR PERFORMANCE!** You have to understand and accept this truth! Your chance for the "abundant life" hinges on your receiving it.

Every time the enemy sneers, "You're so unworthy,"

repeat to him Romans 8:32. Personalize the verse by saying "me" instead of "us": *"Since he did not spare even his own Son for us but gave him up for us all, won't he also surely give us everything else?"* (TLB).

When we ask God to fulfill His promises, He does not rate our worthiness, or shake His head like a bank loan officer and say, "Sorry, you don't have quite enough credit for that promise." No! When you ask God to fulfill His Word the answer is an unqualified, "Yes!"

No promise is dependent upon your performance!

Although we do not obligate God's grace by the way we live, there are benefits to living life by God's laws. What we sow, we will certainly reap. Even though wearing a seat belt does not get you any special consideration from the hospital, in an automobile accident, it might save your life or keep you from going there. Living by God's laws is the highest and best way for a person to live. It will save you endless heartache but it will *not* buy you special merit with God.

God's grace does not neutralize the law of sowing and reaping. The things we do with our money, the way we handle our relationships, and what we do in every other aspect of our life brings a "crop" of results. The negative things in our lives often result from what we have sowed, and are unrelated to God's grace or His attitude of love toward us. Those consequences are the result of choices *we* have made and actions *we* have taken.

The "good news" is that grace can intervene to cause

a crop failure of the negative things we have sown, change results, and even restore things that have been lost because of past mistakes! You do not have to give up on relationships, dreams, or anything that has been lost to you because of the work of the enemy in your life, past sins, or mistakes. You do not have to accept those losses as punishments for things you have done wrong. God has promised that by His grace, you can have them back:

> *And I will restore to you the years that the locust hath eaten, the cankerworm, and the caterpiller, and the palmerworm,...* (Joel 2:25).

This promise was not only given to you but to the children of Israel after they returned from a time of slavery which resulted from their turning from God and worshipping idols. God shows His great mercy to the ones He loves in this promise. Although Israel had sinned greatly against Him and *deserved* to lose everything, in His great mercy, God promised to *restore* what they had lost. This promise holds true for you, too. God will restore to you that which has been lost.

Greasy Grace and Hollow Holiness

> *...Shall we continue in sin, that grace may abound? God forbid. How shall we, that are dead to sin, live any longer therein?* (Romans 6:1,2).

> *For the love of Christ compels us, because we judge thus: that if One died for all, then*

*all died; and He died for all, that those who
live should live no longer for themselves, but
for Him who died for them and rose again*
(II Corinthians 5:14,15 NKJ).

Like prison house lawyers, Christian opportunists
believe that grace is a legal loophole that protects them
when they sin. "Greasy grace" is saying in your heart, "I
know God doesn't want me to do this thing but after I do
it I'll ask His forgiveness. Everything will be all right" or
"I can do anything I want to do, and God will 'freely give
me all things.'"

When you come to really understand that God's love
is so great that He sent His own Son to die for your sins,
you *must* love Him in return. When you love God, you want
to please Him. Jesus said in John 14:15, *"If you love Me, you
will keep My commandments"* (NAS).

When I was growing up, my mother often told me
that she did not want me to smoke cigarettes because my
father was a heavy smoker. She would add, "I don't believe
you will ever smoke. I have confidence in you that you won't
smoke." When the time came that my friends began to smoke
and encouraged me to try smoking, I just could not do it.
Every time I was tempted to smoke, I could hear my mother
saying, "I trust that you will never smoke." Her love
constrained me from smoking. I could not bring myself to
disappoint her.

It is the same with us in our relationship with God.
When we realize how greatly God loves us and how much He
has given to liberate us from sin, we don't want to disappoint
Him by consciously sinning. God admonishes us, *"...Be holy
because I, the LORD your God, am holy"* (Leviticus 19:2 NIV).

Remember the story of Joseph, the son of Jacob, and the coat of many colors? When his jealous brothers sold him into slavery in Egypt, he was taken into the house of Potiphar, the Pharoah's right-hand man. Joseph was such a capable manager that soon he was the chief administrator of Potiphar's household. One day, when Potiphar was away from home, his wife tried to seduce Joseph. Joseph's reply was, "...*How then could I do such a wicked thing and sin against God?*" (Genesis 39:9 NIV).

Joseph was undoubtedly tempted to sin. Pleasing God was more important to him than a few moments of illicit pleasure. When you understand the depth of God's grace and love for you. When you recognize the extent to which He has gone to save you from a wasted life and a horrible eternity, there develops within you a profound gratefulness toward God and a desire to be pleasing to Him. Then when tempted to sin, you will ask, "How could I disappoint the One Who loves me and has done so much for me?"

You Blew It—*Now* What?

> ...*for the LORD your God is gracious and merciful, and will not turn His face from you if you return to Him* (II Chronicles 30:9 NKJ).

Adam and Eve had the ultimate "good life." They lived in a paradise. They had everything they wanted and needed. They even had God as a friendly neighbor who came by their house to socialize. Every animal was subject to them. God had provided Adam the perfect companion and helpmate in Eve. The fruit from hundreds of trees in the Garden of Eden was on their menu; in fact, God withheld from them the fruit of only one tree: the tree of the knowledge of good and evil.

God had anticipated and fulfilled every need of Adam and Eve. Yet, in spite of all the good things in their lives, Adam and Eve fell for the enemy's lie and sinned. However, that did not end God's love and grace toward them. Although they had to bear the consequences of sin, God did not turn His back but showed that He still loved and cared for them by providing for their basic need of clothing. Even then, God was a "cover" for them.

You may remember that the Israelites turned away from God and began to serve idols. After repeated warnings, God allowed them to be taken into captivity by Babylon. Even though they had turned their backs upon God and sacrificed their children upon the altars of demons, God did not turn His back upon them. Rather, He outlined for them how long they would be in captivity and reassured them that He would bring them back to the Promised Land.

> *This is what the LORD says: "When seventy years are completed for Babylon, I will come to you and fulfill my gracious promise to bring you back to this place.* **For I know the plans I have for you," declares the LORD, "plans to prosper you and not to harm you, plans to give you hope and a future"** (Jeremiah 29:10,11 NIV).

God even went on to promise:

*And I will make an everlasting covenant with them, that **I will not turn away from doing them good**; but I will put My fear in their hearts so that they will not depart from Me. Yes, I will rejoice over them to do them good,...*" (Jeremiah 32:40,41 NKJ).

If you have taken the wrong path and have "blown it," God does not hate you; He *still* loves you and has a wonderful plan for your life. Even if you have lived a terrible life for many years like the children of Israel, your gracious heavenly Father will not turn away from you or hate you. He does not want to harm you; He wants to prosper you, give you hope, and do well by you. Put your faith in God, not in your past behavior.

When Satan Wins

...When he lies, he speaks his native language, for he is a liar and the father of lies (John 8:44 NIV).

> Satan
> wins
> when we fall
> for
> his lies.

Why did Eve fall for Satan's lie concerning God's goodness? Why did Job almost give in to the lie? Why didn't the generation of Israelites who escaped from Egypt enter the Promised

Land? Why don't people tithe? Why do so many Christians feel they must earn God's grace?

All of these questions have the same answer. The persons in question believed a lie and did not trust in God's grace or goodness.

The serpent told Eve:

For God knows that when you eat of it your eyes will be opened, and you will be like God, knowing good and evil (Genesis 3:5 NIV).

Instead of believing that God had given them the best of their world, Eve became convinced that God had withheld something good, namely wisdom. She decided to take it for herself.

Eve did not doubt that God had been good to them, but she doubted the depth of His goodness. She thought He could have done more, and resolved to *provide for herself what God had failed to supply*. Christians often do the same thing. Satan subtly tempts Christians to "help God" fulfill their prayers by taking for themselves the thing for which they've prayed. Beware this trick of the enemy! If you are not receiving an answer to a prayer, there is a reason. Do not take things into your own hands; seek God to find out why your prayers are going unanswered.

I know of people who prayed and asked God for a mate. When "Mister or Miss Right" did not come immediately into their lives, these persons "helped God" by finding someone on their own. The result was always disastrous, and in many cases led to years of heartache—and sometimes divorce.

Job was a great man upon the earth and a big man

with God. God was very proud of Job and even bragged to Satan:

> *...Have you considered my servant Job? There is no one on earth like him; he is blameless and upright, a man who fears God and shuns evil"* (Job 1:8 NIV).

You know the story I am sure: Satan challenged God's statement. He declared that Job only loved God because of the blessing and protection upon his life. To prove that His servant was "upright," God allowed Satan to remove the blessings from Job's life.

At the onset of his difficulties, Job declared his belief in God's goodness and integrity by saying,

> *...Naked came I out of my mother's womb, and naked shall I return thither: the LORD gave, and the LORD hath taken away; blessed be the name of the LORD* (Job 1:21).

The Bible says in all this, Job did not sin.

Job's friends challenged his righteousness, claiming he must have sinned to bring such misery upon himself. Job, however, knew that he was righteous before God and had not sinned, but he mismanaged his defense by falling into self-pity. Although he never cursed God, during his response to the attack of his "friends," Job sinned. Finally, God spoke, showing Job and his friends His goodness and their error.

The story of Job illustrates a pitfall Christians must avoid: questioning the goodness of God when "bad things happen to good people." When something bad happens to you, it can cause you to doubt the goodness of God.

First, we must recognize that evil *never* comes from God. Second, we should remember that God's ways are higher than our ways. Although we *may* come to understand why God allows some unfortunate things to happen to us, we will probably *never* fully understand all the reasons until we get to heaven. Sometimes, we must take a leap of faith based upon the fact that we know God is good and deeply loves us.

> *...You have heard of the perseverance of Job and seen the end intended by the Lord— that* **the Lord is very compassionate and merciful** (James 5:11 NKJ).

We may have to say; "God, I don't understand why You allowed this thing to happen. However, I know beyond a doubt that You are good and that You love me and that somehow, some way, You will make *even this* terrible thing turn out for my good and Your glory." *If you fail to recognize God's goodness, Satan will win.* You cannot cover over or choose to forget about negative feelings about God. When you become angry or offended with God, you *must* resolve it or it will cause you to fall away. Remember, the devil's principal stratagy is to make you doubt God's integrity.

The children of Israel witnessed many, many miracles, yet failed to believe that God was good enough to fulfill His promise of providing them a new homeland! He had miraculously set them free from bondage, given them the wealth of their slavemasters, provided food from the heavens and water when there was none to be had. God had protected them from fierce tribes that wanted to kill them, and even prevented their clothing and shoes from wearing out. Yet, in spite of all the supernatural protection and provisions they had seen God furnish, this generation of Israelites missed out on God's best. They failed to believe that God could give them victory over the tribes that inhabited their promised land. Incredible, isn't it?

We would never have made such an obvious mistake, right? On the other hand, how many of us have seen God's supernatural provision in one area of our life, yet failed to believe and receive the victory He had for us in another set of circumstances?

Is there something in your life that seems too hard for God? Is there a situation where *your fear* is bigger than *your faith*? Is there a circumstance that appears to be too great for God's grace? Do not miss out on the abundant life you have been promised. Do not allow yourself to believe that anything is too vast, or too difficult for God. Nothing from your past or your present can separate you from God's love and the power of His grace to meet your need. Do not allow *anything* to keep you from your "promised land."

Just as God took the Children of Israel out of the desert into their Promised Land, He will take you through the sand storm of your dilemma into *your* promised blessing. God has an "intended end" for your crisis:

> ...*You have heard of the perseverance of Job
> and seen **the end intended** by the Lord...*
> (James 5:11 NKJ).

Pitiful Peter the Disastrous Disciple

But when he had turned about and looked on his disciples, he rebuked Peter, saying, Get thee behind me, Satan: for thou savourest not the things that be of God, but the things that be of men (Mark 8:33).

When we think of Peter the apostle, we tend to remember his triumphs and the many times God used him in miraculous ways. Often we forget the rough fisherman Simon Barjona whom Jesus called to be His disciple—Simon, a man *only* God-looking-through-the-eyes-of-grace would consider calling to be a disciple.

When Jesus called Simon Peter to be a disciple, Jesus wanted to reward Peter and give him a great catch of fish—Peter resisted. After preaching to the multitudes from Peter's boat, Jesus told Peter to launch the boat out into the deepest part of Lake Genneserat and put down his net for a big catch. Peter argued, "But, Lord, we fished all night and didn't catch a thing!" He was probably thinking, "I'm a professional fisherman. I worked all night to catch fish and wasn't successful. Are *you*, a carpenter and itinerant preacher, going to tell *me* how to fish? Get real!"

Jesus, though, wasn't interested in getting "real," He wanted to get supernatural! What Jesus meant when He commanded Peter to drop the nets was, "I want to demonstrate my grace, my unearned favor, to you." Begrudgingly, Peter consented and what a surprise he received:

"...But because you say so, I will let down the

*nets." When they had done so, they caught
such a large number of fish that their nets began
to break* (Luke 5:5,6 NIV).

Like Peter, we can get stuck in "natural" thinking and
miss out on God's supernatural blessings.

Later, Peter saw Jesus walking on the water and he
was recklessly determined to do the same thing, but showed
his lack of faith by sinking:

> ..."Come," he said. Then Peter got down out of
> the boat, walked on the water and came toward
> Jesus. But when he saw the wind, he was afraid
> and, beginning to sink, cried out, "Lord, save
> me!" Immediately Jesus reached out his hand
> and caught him. "You of little faith," he said,
> "why did you doubt?" (Matthew 14:30,31 NIV).

In spite of Peter's "lack of faith," Jesus did not give
up on him and say, "Go back to fishing where you belong."
Nor is God going to give up on you when your lack of faith
keeps you from a victory.

Probably Peter's biggest blunder occurred when he tried
to talk Jesus out of dying upon the cross. Peter said, "Never!
I'll never let you go to the cross" and Jesus rebuked him and
said, "...'Get behind me, Satan!..." (Matthew 16:23 NIV). Later,
Peter goofed again when he boasted, "I'll never deny you
Lord! If I have to die, I won't deny you." When the soldiers
came for Jesus, Peter bungled yet again by cutting off
someone's ear.

Jesus was forever cleaning up Peter's messes! Peter
seemed hopeless! How could any good come from Peter the

disastrous disciple? In spite of Peter's mistakes, however, Jesus saw great possibilities in him—and church history proves that Jesus' confidence was well-founded.

If you consider yourself unsuccessful, disadvantaged, inept, undereducated, ungifted, handicapped, underqualified, down and out, learning disabled, or mentally challenged, then Peter is *your* champion. He is a life-sized illustration of a person who was "last" but became "first." In fact, he was a "rock head" who, by God's grace, became the strong boulder upon whom Jesus built His church.

The Rest of the Story

> *And I also say to you that you are Peter, and on this rock I will build My church, and the gates of Hades shall not prevail against it* (Matthew 16:18 NKJ).

On the day of Pentecost when the Holy Spirit was poured out, pitiful Peter became powerful Peter, the first citywide crusade evangelist, as he stood before the multitude and told them about Jesus. That day, Peter, the guy who could never do anything right, had the first of what would prove to be many big altar calls. The Bible says, "*...that day about three thousand souls were added to them*" (Acts 2:41 NKJ).

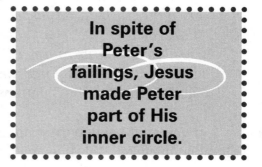

In spite of Peter's failings, Jesus made Peter part of His inner circle.

Peter also started the gentile revival. After receiving the vision of the "unclean" animals and being told by God to eat, Peter understood that salvation was not only for the Jews but also for the gentiles. When invited to preach at the house of Cornelius the Gentile, Peter went eagerly and while he was preaching a revival broke out among the gentiles.

Was Peter forever changed? Would he never blow it again? Unfortunately, Peter was just as human as you and I. While in Antioch working with Paul and the gentiles, he again made a serious mistake, and Paul had to call him to account.

> *When Peter came to Antioch, I opposed him to his face, because he was clearly in the wrong. Before certain men came from James, he used to eat with the Gentiles. But when they arrived, he began to draw back and separate himself from the Gentiles because he was afraid of those who belonged to the circumcision group. The other Jews joined him in his hypocrisy, so that by their hypocrisy even Barnabas was led astray.*
>
> *When I saw that they were not acting in line with the truth of the gospel, I said to Peter in front of them all, "You are a Jew, yet you live like a Gentile and not like a Jew. How is it, then, that you force Gentiles to follow Jewish customs?"* (Galatians 2:11-14 NIV).

Even after being born again and Spirit-filled, we may still make mistakes. Yet, like Peter, God will forgive us and restore our relationship with Him and the plan He has for our lives. The Bible says that the greater our sin, the more grace God sends to assist us: *"...But where sin abounded, grace* [unmerited supernatural favor and blessing] *did much more abound:"* (Romans 5:20).

Peter had not earned the position Jesus gave him in the founding of His Church. Using the Merit System, Peter rated a big zero. But for God's *grace,* this rough, uneducated, uncultured, blue-collar worker would have spent his life working on a fishing boat. However, through Jesus' eyes, the eyes of grace, Peter looked like a pillar of His new Church and that is what he became. When Jesus looks at you, He does not see the zeros, the failures, or mistakes, He sees a person of great value to His kingdom.

Although little is written about Peter after the incident at Antioch, we know that he went on to build a ministry among the Jews similar to Paul's ministry among the gentiles. His legacy is found in two small but precious books of the New Testament—First & Second Peter.

In I Peter 5:10, Peter shares with us what he learned about God's grace:

> And the **God of all grace**, *who called you to his eternal glory in Christ, after you have suffered a little while, **will himself restore you** and make you strong, firm and steadfast* (NIV).

Peter declares that God is the fountain of every kind of grace. He has exactly the type of grace you need for every problem and situation you face. Peter goes on to say that you may suffer for a little while but God will *personally* restore and strengthen you. If you stand firm, God will make you a "steadfast" rock as He did Peter—a person who is not shaken by any circumstance. Peter learned that God's grace was more than sufficient and so can you.

Unlocking Mega-Grace

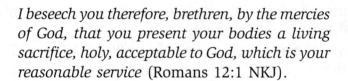

> *I beseech you therefore, brethren, by the mercies of God, that you present your bodies a living sacrifice, holy, acceptable to God, which is your reasonable service* (Romans 12:1 NKJ).

In the story of the rich, young ruler in Matthew 20, Jesus was not asking this young man to just give up his possessions, He was saying, "Give yourself to Me. I want your heart! I want to be first in your life!" Unfortunately, the young man missed mega-grace because he let his possessions take first place in his life.

Jesus said in the Sermon on the Mount:

> *But seek first the kingdom of God and His righteousness, and all these things shall be added to you* (Matthew 6:33 NKJ).

What are you seeking first—prosperity, relationships, security, recognition, pleasure? The list of things we seek after is endless, but we are called to seek *first* only one thing…God. When we make God first in our lives, out of His bottomless heart of love He pours forth rivers of grace, more grace than we expect—and certainly more than we deserve!

John the Baptist said of Jesus:

> *...This was He of whom I said, 'He who comes after me has a higher rank than I, for He existed before me.' For of His fulness we have all received, and* **grace upon grace** *(John 1:15,16 NAS).*

Grace comes through Jesus, and the salvation that He made available to us through the cross. "Grace upon grace" evokes images of waves hitting the shore. We receive one blessing and, before we are even through thanking God for it, another wave of blessing has washed over us! When you put Him first, you will not have to settle for what you *deserve*, you can live a life awash with *grace*—enjoying wave upon wave of blessing.

The 5 Best Ways To...
Not Underestimate the Power of God's Grace

1. To get what you need instead of what you deserve from God—find a promise in the Bible that applies to your situation, ask God to fulfill His Word, and receive your answer by faith through grace. Read John 16:24.

2. Find an Old Testament example of a person who received God's grace even though they didn't "merit" it. (Hint: look at the lives of Job, Abraham, Jacob, Moses, and David.)

3. Pray Joel 2:25, asking God to restore to you what the enemy has

stolen, or what you have lost by your own mistakes.

4. If you've blown it, read the story of the prodigal son found in Luke 15:11-32 —God will take you back!

5. God wants to prosper you in every way—memorize, "Beloved, I pray that you may prosper in all things and be in health, just as your soul prospers" (III John 1:2 NKJ).

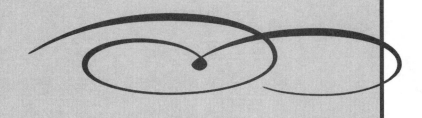

Chapter Two

DISCOVER WHY BAD THINGS HAPPEN TO GOOD PEOPLE

DISCOVER WHY BAD THINGS HAPPEN TO GOOD PEOPLE

Every person at some point in his life looks up to heaven with a broken or angry heart and cries, "Why God, why? Why did you allow this trouble in my life? Why did you let this loved one die? Why did I suffer this financial calamity? How could you allow my marriage to

> *Though He slay me, yet will I trust Him. Even so, I will defend my own ways before Him*
> (Job 13:15 NKJ)

end?" Substituting our individual circumstances, the question we have all asked of God at one time or another is, "Why do the righteous suffer?"

Since earliest times, people have asked the same question, and God *wants* us to understand "why bad things happen to good people." Just as important, God wants us to know what we can do about it when "bad things" happen to us. If you are like me, you've questioned God in your heart about this and you want some concrete answers. The book of Job is devoted to answering these questions.

At first glance, suffering would seem to challenge the legitimacy of God's grace. However, as we watch the story unfold of the world's richest and most famous sufferer, Job, we find that *grace contains the keys to dealing with suffering*. Job learned from his suffering and came out a winner. Since each of us goes through crises, problems, and troubles, we need to learn how Job "bounced back" from his setback of suffering, and how to get over blaming God for our problems. All people, including Christians, have problems—but Christians have provision for their problems.

A Modern-day Tragedy

A young mother had just returned from a day of skiing with her girlfriend. Before she could get her coat off, the telephone rang. When she answered, an unemotional voice informed her, "Your husband is dead."

The man from the morgue went on to ask, "Would you come and identify the body?"

Her voice rising in shock and fear, the young woman responded, "You're lying to me...this is a terrible joke!"

The wooden voice paused for the space of a breath, then said, "Lady, this is no joke; just call the police."

The police verified that it was true. Her husband—the father of their four young children—was dead from gun shot wounds. When she arrived at the morgue, she saw the horrifying sight of her dearly loved husband, riddled with bullet holes, covered with blood, and surrounded by a litter of bottles and tubes.

Later she related to me, "I remember sitting on the divan with the four kids, all crying...one boy in the sixth grade, one boy in the fifth grade, and another boy and girl in the first grade. I was absolutely numb. I knew we had no money, or very little, and I didn't know how in the world I could raise four kids by myself."

However, raise them she did—because the same God

who brought Job through his problems is available today. God walked with her through every step of her time of trial. Now she counsels others concerning the goodness and love of God, boldly declaring, "God is merciful and full of grace."

Job Who?

There was a man in the land of Uz, whose name was Job; and that man was blameless and upright, and one who feared God and shunned evil. And seven sons and three daughters were born to him. Also, his possessions were seven thousand sheep, three thousand camels, five hundred yoke of oxen, five hundred female donkeys, and a very large household, so that this man was the greatest of all the people of the East (Job 1:1-3 NKJ).

To interpret this book and extract its truths, we need to understand the cultural setting of the times. Many believe Job was the first book of the Bible to be written, some 1,500 years before Christ. It is thought that Job lived sometime between Abraham's day and the founding of Israel. According to Hebrew tradition, the story of Job was handed down orally from previous generations, and was written by Moses after his father-in-law, Jethro, told him Job's testimony. It is written in an ancient, elegant form of poetry.

Job was an actual person, and during his life was considered the greatest and wealthiest man of the East. He was immensely wealthy and blessed. He had thousands of head of livestock, miles of grazing land, and countless acres of fields devoted to agriculture. He also had a great household of servants and ten adult children—seven sons and three daughters. In addition, Job was a godly, generous, and wise man who despised evil.

Job scrupulously lived by the spiritual knowledge that he possessed, and took seriously his position as priest for his family. He often prayed for his children and got up early to offer blood sacrifices for their sins. This showed that he believed that the blood of his sacrifices would cover their sins and that there was grace with God for his family and himself through the blood.

There *Will* Be War

> ...*choose you this day whom ye will serve;...as for me and my house, we will serve the LORD* (Joshua 24:15).

When Job is described in Job 1:1-3, the first thing mentioned is his character—"blameless and upright." Next, his family is described. His wealth is spoken of last. The order is important because it clearly shows what things were most important in Job's life. During the course of this true story, we see two forces at war for Job's *character:* God and Satan. The other elements, his family and fortune, become devices and, ultimately, casualties of Satan's attack.

The same kind of conflict continues today. The enemy wants *your* soul, and to get it, he will attack your character, because *character is the personality of the soul.* A Christian's

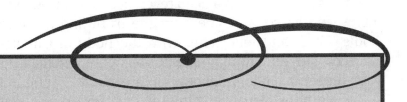

The Land Where Job Lived

"...Two possible locations are Hauran, south of Damascus, and the area between Edom and northern Arabia. The exact location of the land of Uz is unknown, but it was probably east of the Jordan River in the Syrian or Arabian Desert."

(Reprinted by permission from *Nelson's Illustrated Bible Dictionary* © 1986, Thomas Nelson Publishers)

character is based upon a deep reverence for God's goodness, mercy and grace, an esteem for the truth and accuracy of God's Word, and fellowship with the Body of Christ—the Church. The enemy may attack your core beliefs through your family, friends, finances, or career.

Perhaps you are thinking that you don't want a war with the devil—that peaceful coexistence would be okay. Unfortunately, this war started long before you were born, before the creation of the world, when Satan, the leader of the fallen angels, rebelled against God and eventually enslaved humanity with sin. After suffering an early setback in the Garden of Eden, humankind was re-empowered by virtue of Jesus' sacrifice on the cross to resist and fight this foe.

Now, your only choice is whether to become a casualty or a conqueror. There are no neutral parties in this war; you must take a side:

> *No servant can serve two masters; for either he will hate the one and love the other, or else he will be loyal to the one and despise the other....* (Luke 16:13 NKJ).

A Peek Through Heaven's Keyhole

Now there was a day when the sons of God came to present themselves before the LORD, and Satan also came among them. And the LORD said to Satan, "From where do you come?" So Satan answered the LORD and said, "From going to and fro on the earth,

and from walking back and forth on it"
(Job 1:6,7 NKJ).

The book of Job pulls aside the veil of heaven and gives us a rare, brief glimpse of the spirit realm. The "sons of God," an expression used other places in the Bible, refers to angels. The scene portrayed is of a CEO (God) calling a meeting of senior executives (angels) for an update on the progress of their various projects. Satan, the renegade archangel, is among those called by God to account for their actions.

When it is time for Satan to report, he reveals that he has been "stalking" the earth—he and his demonic forces are restless. In Matthew 12:43 (NKJ), Jesus says that a demon who is cast out of a person, *"...goes through dry places, seeking rest, and finds none."* When you are oppressed by the enemy, you may feel restless. God's nature is peaceful, but Satan's is disordered.

Satan is our deadly enemy and, until we are born into the kingdom of God, we are defenseless against his evil. However, after we become God's children, we have God-given power and authority over Satan's schemes against our character, our lives, and the lives of others. In speaking of our power and authority over Satan and his demons, Jesus explains in Luke 10:19:

> *Behold, I give unto you power to tread on serpents and scorpions, and over all the power of the enemy: and nothing shall by any means hurt you.*

Satan is a depraved god. Although he is behind all

the evil on the earth, he has limited powers. Unlike God, Satan is not omniscient (all-knowing), omnipotent (all- powerful), or omnipresent (everywhere at the same time). Later, we will see that God limited Satan's attack and allowed him to go only so far in violating Job. However, Satan is more powerful than a natural person, and only when God enables us with supernatural power can we prevail over him. Satan is a wily opponent, devious and well organized:

> *For our struggle is not against flesh and blood,*
> *but against the rulers, against the authorities,*
> *against the powers of this dark world and*
> *against the spiritual forces of evil in the*
> *heavenly realms* (Ephesians 6:12 NIV).

Grace Talks, the Devil Walks

And the LORD said unto Satan, Hast thou considered my servant Job, that there is none like him in the earth, a perfect and an upright man, one that feareth God, and escheweth evil? (Job 1:8).

When God spoke of Job as "My servant," He was saying to Satan, "Job is mine and not yours." God says the same thing about you and me—but He can say something more about us. Because of Jesus and the cross, we are adopted children of God. We are a part of His family: *"The Spirit himself testifies with our spirit that we are God's children"* (Romans 8:16 NIV). Because of our adoption, we have a better relationship with God than any Old Testament person could have had. When God looks at you through grace, He goes beyond calling you "My servant," and calls you "My son or daughter—My friend." Jesus said:

> *I no longer call you servants, because a servant does not know his master's business. Instead, I have called you friends, for everything that I learned from my Father I have made known to you* (John 15:15 NIV).

You can hear the pride in God's voice as he boasts to Satan, "There isn't anybody like Job on the earth; he's blameless; he's upright, and he fears God and shuns evil." Job sounds like a perfect person.

Was Job perfect? Had Job reached that pinnacle of perfection where he never sinned or did anything wrong? Was he as good as God said? Job was human, and every human has his or her weaknesses. God was speaking through grace when He said Job was "perfect." When God looks at us, He also sees us through the eyes of grace. As a Christian, God sees you at your best, as the person He created you to become.

When Satan responded to God's boast, you will notice that he could not challenge God's grace statement that Job was "perfect." The best Satan could do was throw dust in the air by challenging Job's character—his motives for being good.

Satan is called the accuser of the brethren, but Satan has the same problem with you that he had with Job. Because

To Fear God

"The fear of God reigning in his [Job's] heart was the principle that governed his whole conversation. This made him perfect and upright, inward and entire for God, universal and uniform in religion; this kept him close and constant to his duty. **He feared God, had a reverence for his majesty, a regard to his authority, and a dread of his wrath.**"

(From *Matthew Henry's Commentary*)

of grace, your past, forgiven sins are irrelevant to God. Satan would be laughed out of heaven for bringing your "forgiven sins" up before your Father. The only thing Satan can insinuate to God about you is the *un*forgiven sin in your life. To be un-accuse-able, repent of your sin, turn away from it, get it under the blood of Christ, and no longer make a place for it in your life:

> *If we confess our sins, He is faithful and just*
> *to forgive us our sins and to cleanse us from*
> *all unrighteousness* (I John 1:9 NKJ).

In fact, the only person who will listen to Satan's talk about your past sins is *you.* Wake up and see yourself as God sees you—"blameless"! Put the past where it belongs—behind you. Stop tolerating Satan's put-downs! When Satan reminds you of your past sins, remind him of Jesus' shed blood that covers your sins, and he will have to "take a walk."

Know Your Enemy

> *...in order that Satan might not outwit us.*
> *For we are not unaware of his schemes*
> (II Corinthians 2:11 NIV).

Since we are involved in a war and have an enemy who wants to destroy our soul and attack our character just as much as he did Job's, we need to know who Satan is and understand his methods.

Satan and the angels who followed him were created

before the earth. In fact, Satan was created as one of the few, super-powerful archangels. The Bible says Satan was the most beautiful of God's angels and the leader of worship. However, Satan let pride enter his heart. He decided to overthrow God. The Bible goes on to tell how Satan was thrown out of heaven with about one-third of the heavenly host, whom he had corrupted and convinced to join his conspiracy against God.

Since his expulsion from heaven, Satan has attempted to steal what God loves the most: His creation—the earth and the people on it. Once sin entered the world when Satan beguiled Eve, Satan determined the realm of earth to be *his* kingdom, and all mankind his slaves.

Satan did not get away with his rebellion against God. He was tried in the courts of heaven, judged, found guilty, and sentenced to eternal damnation (see Isaiah 14:12-15). However, because the sentence has yet to be carried out, our world is in the grip of a sadistic, cruel being who would like nothing better than to steal from you, kill you, and destroy those things and people most precious to you. That is why our world is in such a deplorable condition and why "bad things happen to good people." Satan, the demon god, wants to taint your character...steal your soul...and rob you of your life.

Satan is a powerful being who can influence people's thoughts. He holds the power of death. In the Bible, he is called the prince of the power of the air, a murderer, the father of lies, and has many other chilling titles. Do not overrate Satan—but don't underestimate him, either!

Satan's Challenge

"Does Job fear God for nothing?" Satan replied. "Have you not put a hedge around him and his household and everything he has? You have blessed the work of his hands, so that his flocks and herds are spread throughout the land. But stretch out your hand and strike everything he has, and he will surely curse you to your face." The LORD said to Satan, "Very well, then, everything he has is in your hands, but on the man himself do not lay a finger." Then Satan went out from the presence of the LORD (Job 1:9-12 NIV).

Satan responded to the pride God had in His servant by saying that Job's character and motives for serving God were flawed, and that Job's love for God was "bought" by God's goodness to him. This statement challenged both Job's and God's honor. God could not sit idly by and allow Satan to cast aspersions on His character. That is the reason God allowed this test to take place. If, indeed, Job was serving God only because he was selfish, it meant he was not a "righteous" man but a hypocrite. If God accepted the worship of a hypocrite, then He Himself was not righteous.

When God accepted the devil's challenge, it instigated a trial of unimaginable importance and sweeping significance. It was a duel of honor to vindicate *both* Job and God. Think of the confidence God put in His servant Job. The vindication of God's *own* character was in Job's very human hands! To prove Satan wrong, God gave him liberty to remove the benefits that Job's righteous living had brought to him. He trusted implicitly that Job would continue to love and worship Him, in bad times as well as good.

It is vital that we understand who it was that attacked Job's family and destroyed his possessions. The perpetrator was not God but Satan. It is *always* Satan, never God, who causes "bad things to happen to good people." Satan's method of attack against Job took the form of fast, hard punches: the loss of Job's donkeys, sheep, and camels, and finally—the knockout blow—the death of his children. Satan was certain Job would drop to the canvas and curse God, but he was in for a surprise.

Devastation Strikes

...a messenger came to Job and said, "The oxen were plowing and the donkeys were grazing nearby, and the Sabeans attacked and carried them off. They put the servants to the sword, and I am the only one who has escaped to tell you!"

While he was still speaking, another messenger came and said, "The fire of God fell from the sky and burned up the sheep and the servants, and I am the only one who has escaped to tell you!"

While he was still speaking, another messenger came and said, "The Chaldeans formed three raiding parties and swept down on your camels and carried them off. They put the servants to the sword, and I am the only one who has escaped to tell you!"

While he was still speaking, yet another messenger came and said, "Your sons and daughters were feasting and drinking wine at the oldest brother's house, when suddenly a mighty wind swept in from the desert and struck the four corners of the house. It collapsed on them and they are dead, and I am the only one who has escaped to tell you!" (Job 1:14-19 NIV).

Within the space of a few moments, Job went from the "man who has everything" to a street-person who lives at the city dump. Not only were his possessions gone but, most devastating of all, his beloved children were dead. Satan loves to target our characters by causing us to question God's goodness and grace after giving us the "shock treatment:" not just one calamity or problem, but many at the same time. Have you noticed that bad things often come in multiples? Rarely is it just one thing that goes wrong— more often several calamities occur at once. When problems turn up one or even two at a time, there's a good chance we may be able to handle them, but Satan knows that when *everything* goes wrong at the *same time*, we can easily be overwhelmed.

Doesn't it seem coincidental that in each of these disasters a single person was left alive to bring Job the bad news? This is another device of the devil: send a first-hand witness to deliver a bad report. Just as God uses people to bring blessing into your life, the enemy uses people to bring the opposite.

Although Satan uses people, do not make the mistake of thinking that people are your enemy. Your real enemy is the devil:

> *For our struggle is not against flesh and blood, but against the rulers, against the authorities, against the powers of this dark world and against the spiritual forces of evil in the heavenly realms* (Ephesians 6:12 NIV).

Job fell to the ground in worship!

How did Job handle this devastating news? Did he lose his character along with everything else as Satan had predicted? Let's watch closely what Job did and said. The Bible says that Job got up, tore his robe, shaved his head, and fell to the ground (signs of mourning in his culture). What Job did while on the ground decided his destiny. What you do when you are knocked to the ground by your problems will decide yours as well.

There is no question that Satan had knocked Job *down*—but had he knocked him *out*? Would Job blame God for his misfortune, curse Him and die? Would he whine...writhe in emotional pain... moan in mental anguish...cringe in fear...

or faint in defeat? No, *Job fell to the ground in worship!* Amazing! After the loss of his children and possessions—everything he held dear—the Bible says that Job *worshipped* God:

> *And he said: 'Naked I came from my mother's womb, and naked shall I return there. The LORD gave, and the LORD has taken away; blessed be the name of the LORD'* (Job 1:21 NKJ).

God's confidence in this "righteous man" was well placed!

From Bad to Worse

> *"Skin for skin!" Satan replied. "A man will give all he has for his own life. But stretch out your hand and strike his flesh and bones, and he will surely curse you to your face." The LORD said to Satan, "Very well, then, he is in your hands; but you must spare his life." So Satan went out from the presence of the LORD and afflicted Job with painful sores from the soles of his feet to the top of his head* (Job 2:4-7 NIV).

As the story proceeds, God again calls the angels to report, and Satan's attendance is again required. God once more proudly points out Job's virtues to Satan, reminding him that, in spite of his trials, Job still maintains his integrity. Though he'd lost the first round, Satan did not give up, but struck out again at Job's integrity. This time there was a difference—"Skin for skin!" Believing Job would surely abandon God if the loss was more personally painful, Satan cursed Job with terrible boils. He presumed Job would lose his faith and curse God to His face.

Notice that Satan did not give up after one attack on Job. He won't stop with one attack on you, either. Remember when Jesus went into the wilderness and was "tempted" by Satan? Jesus wasn't tempted only once, but suffered several temptations. Finally, the Bible says:

> *And when the devil had ended all the temptation, he departed from him for a season* (Luke 4:13).

Your temptation, trial, or crisis *will not* continue endlessly. The Bible says that angels came and ministered to Jesus. God will do the same for you. He promises that your trials *will* end, and that God himself will heal and comfort you:

> *...the Father of compassion and the God of all comfort, who comforts us in all our troubles, so that we can comfort those in any trouble with the comfort we ourselves have received from God* (II Corinthians 1:3,4 NIV).

To disprove Satan's contentions that Job served God for selfish reasons, God gave the devil permission to mistreat (but not destroy) Job's body. Make note again, *God did not cause Job's sickness.* Neither does he make you sick. Jesus, Who was sent to destroy the works of the devil and to set free those whom Satan had bound,

"[Sore boils]...

Bishchiyn, 'with an evil inflammation.' What this diabolical disorder was, interpreters are not agreed. Some think it was the leprosy, and this is the reason why he dwelt by himself, and had his habitation in an unclean place, without the city, or in the open air: and the reason why his friends beheld him afar off, was because they knew that the disorder was infectious.

His scraping himself with a potsherd indicates a disease accompanied with intolerable itching, one of the characteristics of the smallpox.... In the elephantiasis and leprosy there is, properly speaking, no boil or detached inflammation, or swelling, but one uniform disordered state of the whole surface, so that the whole body is covered with loathsome scales, and the skin appears like that of the elephant thick and wrinkled, from which appearance the disorder has its name. In the smallpox, it is different; each pock or pustule is a separate inflammation, tending to suppuration; and during this process, the fever is in general very high, and the anguish and distress of the patient intolerable. When the suppuration is pretty far advanced, the itching is extreme and the hands are often obliged to be confined to prevent the patient from literally tearing his own flesh.

(From *Adam Clarke Commentary*)

healed multitudes of people—even those who persecuted Him—*but not even in a single instance* did Jesus ever make someone suffer.

After Satan cursed Job with painful, itching boils, Job withdrew to a dump outside the city. There, among the garbage, dung, and ashes, he took his sad place. Just days before, Job had been welcomed to the chair of highest honor at the city's gate. What a contrast to find him slouched, miserable and diseased, outside the gate upon a mount of trash, scratching his intolerably itching boils with a scrap of pottery!

Helpmate?

I used to wonder why Satan didn't cause Job's wife to die. After all, Satan had mercilessly robbed Job of his beloved children—why not kill the whole family and leave Job entirely alone? After carefully reading the episode in which Job's wife comes to talk to her husband, I believe Satan let her live because he had a purpose for her. He found a "loophole" in her character that would allow him to use her for his own evil ends.

What a help and encouragement Job's wife could have been to her suffering husband! She could have given him comfort and made his loss so much easier to bear had she been supportive. Instead, she uttered with venom, *"...'Are you still holding on to your integrity? Curse God and die!'"* (Job 2:9 NIV).

Satan found a way to use "Mrs. Job" to deliver one final, devastating blow. This was truly the lowest moment of Job's personal ruination. Everything from his former "good life" was now gone—his children, his wealth, and finally his wife. She had become the accomplice of Satan in trying to rob Job of his integrity—and she obviously wanted him dead.

Maybe Job's worldly wife was embarrassed to be associated with a loser like Job. Perhaps she thought she was making a humane suggestion for euthanasia. Whatever her reasons, her words could not have been more devastating to a man trying to hang on to his belief in a just, fair, and loving God. Sometimes, Satan will attack you through the person who is closest and dearest to you, knowing that person can wound you the most.

To his credit, Job did not cave in to this latest distress. He could have agreed with his wife, or ignored her. Instead Job rebuked her and said:

> ...*'You are talking like a foolish woman. Shall we accept good from God, and not trouble?' In all this, Job did not sin in what he said* (Job 2:10 NIV).

Despite his physical and spiritual pain, Job took a stand for God's integrity.

Enduring is a Key

> *For you have need of **endurance**, so that after you have done the will of God, you may **receive the promise**:* (Hebrews 10:36 NKJ).

Don't give up! Don't give in! Don't give out! And

please do not get mad at God! He loves you.

One of the keys to bouncing back from your setbacks is *endurance*. There is a reward for enduring, and that reward is *blessing*. Later, we will talk about Job's blessing for persisting, but you need to realize…remember…and take strength from the fact that God has promised that there is *always a reward* for enduring the crises of your life. If you hang on, reject the opportunity to be angry with God, and refuse to become offended with people, God will greatly reward you. If you give up, give in, give out, or get mad, the reward is withheld, and your trials may lengthen.

> Indeed we **count them blessed** who endure.
> You have heard of the perseverance of Job and
> seen the **end intended by the Lord**—that the
> Lord is very compassionate and merciful
> (James 5:11 NKJ)

God has an "intended end" for your troubles, trials, and tribulations. Trials always seem to last a long time when you are going through them, but compared to the scope of your lifetime, they are short. However, the benefit that comes from *enduring* your trial lasts forever. If you will endure, God will use your situation to move you a giant stride forward.

The Big Key—Worship to Win

Remember, the purpose of the attack upon Job was to destroy his character and to gain possession of his soul. The devil did not win just by taking away Job's wealth or by killing his children. Satan has no interest in those things. Satan's victory could come only if Job allowed his character to weaken. Then Job would lose the final and most important thing—his soul. Satan attacks us for exactly the same reason: he wants our souls.

When we are going through a trial or attack, quite naturally we focus upon our loss. However, we can become so absorbed in our crisis, that we don't have a clue what is *really* going on, what is the root cause and real reason for our situation. *Wake up!* Things are not what they seem. It's your character that is really under attack. The issue isn't what you've lost—God can restore that to you just as He did for Job. The *real* issue is how you react to your loss. What will you do? Will you blame God or, like Job, will you continue to worship Him?

When a bad thing happens in your life, you haven't yet lost (and the devil hasn't yet won) until you *react* to your crisis. *You win or lose in your trial by how you let tragedy affect your character.* How you react to tragedy is what will make you a winner and Satan a loser—or vice versa.

What will you do when, like Job, *you* are grounded by a devastating blow? Will you become angry and blame God? Will you become embittered at the people Satan used against you? Will you conclude that you are a victim and give up? *This is your defining moment.*

There is only one *right* thing to do when a crisis has put your face in the dirt, and that is to worship. In the natural, it sounds ridiculous to worship in a crisis. Instead, we could be doing things—shoring up losses, implementing damage control, doing anything! You may think, "Worship God? That's for Sunday services and besides, He may have been the one who caused my

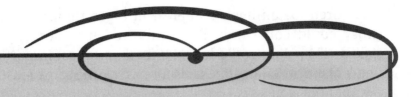

End of the Accuser

*Then I heard a loud voice saying in heaven, "Now salvation, and strength, and the kingdom of our God, and the power of His Christ have come, for **the accuser of our brethren, who accused them before our God day and night, has been cast down."** And they overcame him by the blood of the Lamb and by the word of their testimony, and they did not love their lives to the death* (Revelation 12:10,11 NKJ).

problem in the first place!"

Worshipping God, however, is the most effective thing you can do. When you worship God in the midst of your crises, you are saying as Job did, "God, I trust in your love and goodness, I believe in your grace no matter what happens!" When you worship God during your trials, you are spitting in the eye of Satan and declaring, "I'm going to win and you are going to lose!"

The moment you shove your personal distress aside and begin to worship God, you have won. It shows that you understand that this crisis isn't about what you lost, but about the enemy trying to grind down your *character* and steal your soul. To continue winning, you must resolve to continue worshipping God no matter what happens. It will not come naturally, and you won't feel like you're winning— *but you are.*

Your determination to worship God in your crises will be challenged, but if you want to win...praise Him "anyhow." The devil may bombard you with more troubles to test your resolve, but don't allow them to distract you from your winning strategy—worship. The *real* trial is over once you make the determination to worship God.

God can work anything to your benefit, even your trials and problems. When you begin to focus upon God through worship, He will show you what the enemy is doing, and give you wisdom about steps you can take to win in your situation.

How do you endure your problems? You endure through worship. Worship transfuses your weak and beaten down spirit with an injection of God's power and strength. The hardest time to worship God is in the middle of a crisis— but the effort is well worth it because your "sacrifice of praise" brings a promise of blessing and restoration:

> *'...and of those who will bring the sacrifice of praise into the house of the LORD. For I will cause the captives of the land to return as at the first,' says the LORD* (Jeremiah 33:11 NKJ).

Worship, according to Psalms, is our ticket into the throne room of God:

> *Enter into his gates with thanksgiving, and into his courts with praise: be thankful unto him, and bless his name. For the LORD is good; his mercy is everlasting; and his truth endureth to all generations* (Psalms 100:4,5).

Once in God's throne room, we can go before the "throne of grace" to find the help (grace) that we need.

What Job Didn't Understand

> *But now He [Jesus] has obtained a more excellent ministry, inasmuch as He is also Mediator of a **better covenant, which was established on better promises*** (Hebrews 8:6 NKJ).

Job did not understand that Satan was the one to blame for his problems. Sometimes we may not understand that either. Think about it: God's nature is love, truth, and honesty, but Satan's is described by Jesus as one who seeks to *"...steal, and to kill, and to destroy:..."* (John 10:10). When you put these two natures in a police lineup, identifying the perpetrator of Job's tragedy is easy. Although Job did not understand that God was not the cause of his calamities, he turned to and worshipped Him anyway. This was a great victory for God and, although Job did not know it, he had won a great victory, too.

We are more fortunate than Job because he did not have the knowledge of God's nature and grace that we have through His Word. Job did not have a Bible. Job knew the minimum about grace. Unfortunately, that is all that many Christians today know: the forgiveness of sin through the blood sacrifice. Job made sacrifices for the sins of his family, and undoubtedly for himself. He knew that because of the shed blood of the sacrifices, God would forgive their sins. Many people today know that they can receive forgiveness of their sins through the blood sacrifice of Jesus on the cross. However, grace goes even further than cleansing sin. Grace also provides for healing, deliverance, miracles, favor, and much more.

When we are faced with trials, we know that we can find the help we need from God to make it through. He is not a far-off observer of our difficulties. Rather, He longs to come near and provide supernatural help to bring us through in great victory:

> *Let us then approach the **throne of grace** with confidence, so that we may receive mercy and find **grace to help us in our time of need*** (Hebrews 4:16 NIV).

Unfortunately, Job and many Christians have yet to discover the "throne of *grace.*"

You are entitled to access God's "grace to help in

time of need." This grace is whatever kind of help you need for your dilemma. If you are sick, you can have healing grace. If you are battling with an addiction, you can have grace for deliverance. If you are struggling financially, you can call upon financial grace. Whatever your need, God has "manifold grace" to meet it (see I Peter 4:10).

Character Wars

In this you greatly rejoice, even though now for a little while, if necessary, you have been distressed by various trials, that the proof of your faith, being more precious than gold which is perishable, even though tested by fire, may be found to result in praise and glory and honor at the revelation of Jesus Christ; (I Peter 1:6,7 NAS).

We have discovered that Job's trials were a battle for his "character." In addition, we've found that the prize in the "character war" was Job's soul, and that Satan is fighting the same war for our lives today. Satan's attacks are aimed at weakening and perverting our characters to get our souls.

Satan sees trials as a war to weaken and destroy us, but God can purify and enhance us through them. Throughout the Bible, the trials of life are compared to fire. In ancient times, fire was used to purify. Heating with fire purifies metals. Putting gold into a crucible (a container) and heating it is a way to purify gold. Because various materials have different melting or burning temperatures, as the gold becomes hotter, some waste products burn off and others rise to the top as dross, or waste, to be scooped out of the molten gold. After firing and removing extraneous materials, the remaining gold is very pure, which makes it more precious.

You are like a nugget of gold. When you are born again, you are like a nugget just mined from the ground with bits of dirt and impurities still clinging to it. God has a specific place for that nugget of gold, which is you. However, if you are to shine, be successful, and know the joy of being in that perfect place, then, like the nugget, you need to be purified and molded into a useful shape.

One of God's methods for getting rid of the extraneous things that keep you from achieving all that you can be in His kingdom are the "trials of life." God does not cause your trials, but He uses them for His purposes.

Several years ago, a woman who was a sweet, godly Christian joined our congregation. She was very active in the church, but her husband would never attend church with her. He liked sports and being outdoors and was indifferent to her involvement in spiritual things. In fact, he showed little attention to her at all. A handsome, single evangelist came to the church, and he showed a lot of interest in her. His attraction had to have been extremely tempting for her. She could have thought, "I'll dump my pathetic-excuse-for-a-husband and hook up with this powerful man of God, and we will have a great ministry together." However, she did not get involved with him, but stayed faithful to her "inattentive" husband.

Finally, she and her husband had a child, and the husband ignored the child in the same way. God's hand was upon the woman's life, and He called her into full-time ministry. Her husband, true to form, could have cared less about her call to ministry and spent more and more time away from home. After several years of this kind of neglectful treatment, she felt the Lord prompt her to say, "I'm not going to continue living with you like this. You don't support us. You don't want to serve God, and you're unhappy with me because I do want to serve Him. I'm going to leave you because I don't believe that you want a godly life or that you want to take responsibility for your family."

Within three weeks, her husband was saved and Spirit-filled. He became turned-on to God, and today he is an important part of her nationwide ministry. Her daughter is serving God and also feels called into ministry. This woman endured many years of a bad marriage. She did not take the easy way out. She was patient and faithful to the Lord. She believed that God had an "expected end" for her trial and she refused to write the end to her own story. She left it in God's hands.

The "Intended End"—Your Promotion

> *Indeed we count them **blessed who endure**. You have heard of the perseverance of Job and seen the **end intended by the Lord**—that the Lord is very compassionate and merciful* (James 5:11 NKJ).

If you worship, endure, and seek God during your trials, He will reward you with a promotion. James 5:11 calls it an "intended" end. God had an "intended" end for Job. He not only received a double portion of material blessings, but Job came out of his trials a great intercessor.

In Ezekiel 14:14-22, while talking about a great

judgment that is going to come upon Israel, God lists the three greatest intercessors of the Old Testament and says:

> *...as surely as I live, declares the Sovereign LORD, even if these three men were in it, they could not save their own sons or daughters. They alone would be saved* (Ezekiel 14:18 NIV).

God is saying, "If these three great intercessors were here to pray for you, even they could not save your nation or you—their own descendants—from *this* judgment."

It is not surprising to find Daniel listed as a great intercessor. He prayed the great intercessory prayer that caused his people to return to Israel after spending 70 years as captives in Babylon (see Daniel 9).

Perhaps you have never thought of Noah as one of the great intercessors of the Old Testament, but God does. After the flood and upon leaving the ark, Noah built an altar and made sacrifices to God. With that burnt offering, Noah became the intercessor for the lives of all of mankind yet to come. Out of his intercession, God promised never again to destroy the earth by water, and He gave the rainbow as the visible symbol for His promise.

For many people, the most surprising person named as a great intercessor is Job. However, in the closing chapter of the book of Job, you may recall that God was unhappy with Job's three "comforters," who had come intending to support Job, but instead had been used by Satan to torment him. God required them to make a burnt offering for their sin of "accusing" Job. However, the sacrifice alone was not enough. God said that He would only forgive their sins when Job interceded for them. Through his trials, Job not only learned to worship and endure, but he also learned to intercede.

Soul Prosperity—Turning Inside Out

*Beloved, I pray that you may prosper in all things and be in health, **just as your soul prospers*** (III John 1:2 NKJ).

To keep your soul from becoming discouraged and full of despair during a trial, you must do things that will "prosper" your soul. To come out of your trials a victor, to get God's "jump" to the next level spiritually, physically, or financially, you must prosper in your soul during your trial.

The soul becomes prosperous when it is fed spiritual food—God's truth. A healthy menu for the soul is a balanced diet of prayer, meditation in the Word, and the exhortation of preaching. God's wisdom is like honey in the diet of the soul. God has wisdom you can only learn while you are in a crisis. The connection between soul prosperity and wisdom is explained in Proverbs 3:13,16-18 (NIV):

Blessed is the man who finds wisdom....Long life is in her right hand; in her left hand are riches and honor. Her ways are pleasant ways, and all her paths are peace. She is a tree of life to those who embrace her; those who lay hold of her will be blessed.

During a crisis you will find wisdom's "pleasant way and peaceful paths" like an eye of calm in the midst of your hurricane. A healthy, prosperous soul is one that is consistently being fed God's truth. You have to regularly feed your soul—every day, not just once a week on Sunday.

By constantly filling your mind with God's wisdom, you head off feelings of fear, frustration, guilt, and other negative thoughts that accompany a crisis. During such times, you need God's wisdom the most; so commit to prospering your soul by a daily regimen of prayer and Bible meditation.

When you pursue God's wisdom with all your heart, He will guarantee victory in your soul. The Word will build your faith for a wonderful future and the end to your crisis: *"So then faith comes by hearing, and hearing by the word of God"* (Romans 10:17 NKJ). Nothing may have changed around you, but you will have an assurance on the inside that God is taking you through and giving you the victory. Once the faith for your victory is established on the inside of you, it is only a matter of time before the situation "turns inside out." The victory inside you is manifested on the outside in the circumstances of your life. The crisis is over, and God springboards you to a new level of prosperity in some area of your life.

"Beam Me Up, Lord!"

"Oh, Lord, take me home. Just get me out of here." I think most people at some time or other during a severe predicament have prayed, or at least thought about, asking God to remove their suffering by taking them "home" to heaven. Please hear me: suicide is the *opposite* of soul prosperity and comes out of a soul that is destitute.

God does not answer prayers like that, but He *will*

bring you through your problems when you are depressed, discouraged, and full of despair. Job never cursed God; however, he cursed the day he was conceived and the day he was born, lamenting that he did not die during or after delivery. Clearly, Job wished that he were dead.

When God wanted to slay the children of Israel, Moses—the great shepherd—was the one man who stood between the wrath of God and His people. On that occasion, Moses declared that if God killed the children of Israel, He would have to take him, too. This powerful man of God on another occasion became so weary of the endless complaining of the people that he cried out to God, "I'm tired of these people! Just take me home."

Jonah was the prophet who was swallowed by a huge fish, most believe a whale, when he ran away from God's call to preach repentance to the wicked people of Nineveh. Nineveh was the enemy of the Hebrew people. Jonah disliked Nineveh so much, and wanted to see them destroyed so badly, that after giving in and preaching to Nineveh, and seeing them repent, he was depressed. In despair, he sat outside Nineveh and said, *"Now, O LORD, take away my life, for it is better for me to die than to live"* (Jonah 4:3 NIV).

Elijah "faced down" the prophets of Baal when he challenged them to have their god consume an animal sacrifice by fire. He said to Israel, "The God who answers by fire—let him be your God!" (See I Kings 18:24). The prophets of Baal danced, chanted, and cut themselves, but no fire came to consume their sacrifice. Elijah dumped water upon his sacrifice, prayed one simple prayer, and the fire of God fell and consumed the sacrifice, the wood, the stones— and even licked up the water!

After witnessing this miracle, tens of thousands of Israelites returned to God. It was a day of great victory for Elijah and God. When Jezebel, the unholy queen of Israel, heard about the defeat and deaths of her prophets, she signed Elijah's death warrant. Elijah, overwhelmed with fear, ran away to the mountains. When he got there he said to God, *"...It is enough; now, O LORD, take away my life; for I am not better than my fathers* (I Kings 19:4).

God did not answer these suicide prayers. When we want to end it all, God looks at us as He looked at them, through the eyes of love and grace. He comforts us and says, "Hang on! I've got some great things yet for you to do. This trial will end, and you will be better in the end than you were at the beginning."

When God speaks to you through His Word or through an anointed ministry, your soul begins to prosper, and you learn the things God wants to teach you during your trial. The way to get through depression is not by complaining, being angry with God or others, feeling sorry for yourself, or wanting to give up. It is not the time to jump off a bridge, but to jump into the middle of the river of God's wisdom. Read and meditate upon His Word, so you will get the nourishment your soul needs, and learn what you can do to "prosper in all things" during your crisis.

God has a purpose in the process. God wanted to make Job a great intercessor. He wanted Moses to take His people to the Promised Land. God had more mighty deeds for Elijah to do. God wanted to save a nation through Jonah. If you've failed, given up, or even let people down, don't think that God is finished with you. He *still* forgives. He *still* has great plans for you and wants to do something special and important *for you*—and *through you.*

Devil! Be Gone!

Isn't it interesting how, at one point in Job's story, Satan disappears from the stage? He goes underground, and we see "people" take up the task of tormenting Job. For most of us, the hardest and most difficult trials we face are from other people. Satan employs the same strategy against us, he uses people to get to us—even close friends and family. And so it will continue, until you deal with it, get the victory over it, and bind the devil.

You do not have to put up with Satan's harassment. The Bible teaches that the devil is under your feet. You don't have to be a great prayer warrior, a TV evangelist, or a great man or woman of faith. Jesus says simply and clearly:

> *I have given you authority to trample on snakes and scorpions and to overcome all the power of the enemy; nothing will harm you* (Luke 10:19 NIV).

The "you" in this verse means any born-again believer. "You" could be a new or mature Christian. "You" may be a child or young person. Whoever you are, *you* can step on the devil. Yes, *you* have the authority to stomp the devil into the dirt. *You* have the right to cast him out of your life and your affairs. Say it aloud, "You harassing spirit, in the powerful name of Jesus, I rebuke you and cast you out of this situation. Now *be gone* in Jesus' name!"

Grace Questioned

Question: If you sin, will God retaliate against you and make you sick?

Answer: No, God will not make you sick—but your sin might! When you sin, God is not glaring down at you from heaven, shaking His finger and looking for the best way to punish you. Rather, He is like the father of the prodigal son, waiting with open arms to welcome you back. All you need do is confess your sin, for *"...he is faithful and just to forgive us our sins, and to cleanse us from all unrighteousness* (I John 1:9).

Question: If my faith is not strong enough, will God be angry with me?

Answer: No, God is very kind when we have failures of faith. Recall how long-suffering God was with Job and how Jesus worked with Peter when he had a faith failure. God knows that we are not perfect: *"for he knows how we are formed, he remembers that we are dust"* (Psalms 103:14 NIV). God does not expect us to have "perfect" faith; however, He does expect us to be maturing in faith. Jesus is working in us to perfect our faith:

*Let us fix our eyes on Jesus, **the author and perfecter of our faith**, who for the joy set before him endured the cross, scorning its shame, and sat down at the right hand of the throne of God* (Hebrews 12:2 NIV).

Question: If I cannot conquer repetitive sins in my life, will God withdraw His blessing?

Answer: God is long-suffering. However, we do not know how long He will bless us if we continue to sin. I believe that you are blessed until you go to be with Jesus. However, sin can destroy some of your blessings, and sin that is destructive to your body can kill you. God's grace may arrest all or a part of the harvest of sin, but the real solution is deliverance.

Question: When bad things happen, does it mean that God is mad at me?

Answer: God is not mad at you, even when you're naughty. God's love is not conditional. Jesus suffered horribly on the cross, although He never sinned, and God was certainly not mad at Him. Jesus suffered so that we would not have to suffer. He took to the cross our sins, grief, sorrows, and rejections so that we could live free of those things. When you are born again, the person you were dies and you become new: *"Therefore, if anyone is in Christ, he is a new creation; old things have passed away; behold, all things have become new"* (II Corinthians 5:17 NKJ).

God is not mad at you!

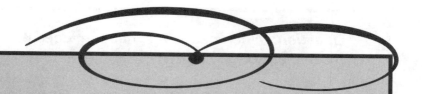

The 5 Best Ways To...
Discover—Why Bad Things Happen to Good People

1. Begin a "blessings journal," in which you record all answers to prayer and all the unexpected "good things" God does for you. When facing a trial, you can read it for encouragement!

2. Don't give up—enduring is a key to succeeding in your circumstance. Learn the reward for "enduring" in James 5:11.

3. Discover the biggest key to overcoming during trials by reading

II Chronicles 20:1-29 and finding out what the priests who went before God's army did to defeat their enemy.

4. God has a promotion for you—an "intended end." Find someone in the Bible, other than Job, who enjoyed a promotion after his crisis. (Hint: look into the life of David and other Old Testament characters.)

5. To confirm your authority to overcome the enemy, read and memorize Luke 10:19.

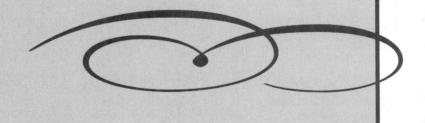

Chapter Three

STOP BLAMING YOURSELF: "HOW COULD I HAVE BEEN SO STUPID?"

STOP BLAMING YOURSELF: "HOW COULD I HAVE BEEN SO STUPID?"

Most of the book of Job is about **The Blame Game**—who is to blame for Job's trials. Job's "comforters" blamed Job, while Job blamed God. The great "blame" debates make up 34 of the 42 chapters of the book of Job.

Affixing blame during a misfortune is one of the tactics Satan uses to distract us from the more important thing—dealing with the situation itself. Anytime a "bad" thing happens, the first thing we feel is the need to figure out whom to blame. It is estimated that the debates in the book of Job lasted for nine months. During that time, Job's friends wagged their fingers in his face and told him, "*You* are to blame for your trials," while Job pointed up to heaven, shook his finger in the face of God, and declared, "God's to blame!" Who was *really* to blame? Satan! Satan, that sly, invisible deceiver was stalking Job.

"The Blame Game" is too dangerous to play. The effort to affix blame caused Job's best friends, men who had known and respected him for years, to slander him and commit sin. To exonerate himself, Job became self-

> *Hear my words, you wise men; listen to me, you men of learning. For the ear tests words as the tongue tastes food. Let us discern for ourselves what is right; let us learn together what is good* (Job 34:2-4 NIV).

righteous, blamed God for his trials, stumbled, and nearly fell prey to Satan. Neither Job nor his friends realized that Satan was at the root of Job's problems. They did not have the understanding necessary to make a judgment, but they judged anyway. Unless we receive a revelation from God during a crisis, we will not have enough information to make a wise judgment, either. We must be careful to avoid this device of the enemy— blaming. Otherwise, we risk having God ask *us* as He did Job: *"Would you discredit my justice? Would you condemn me to justify yourself?"* (Job 40:8 NIV).

For nine months, these friends harassed Job, when the time could have been put to a more constructive use. Had Job's friends not succumbed to the temptation to assign blame, and been distracted from their *real* purpose to comfort him, they could have stood in the gap for Job and perhaps eased his suffering.

The Crippling Burden of Guilt

The burden of guilt for past sins can be crippling. It can cause a negative self-image and a loss of faith. Guilt can even lead to *spiritual* distortion.

While some people remain in denial and never accept blame for the things they have done, a great many people blame themselves for *all* their problems. The fact is, we all make mistakes and, commonly, we do cause many of our own problems. We *should* judge ourselves to determine whether our words and actions are in line with God's Word. We should accept blame for our mistakes and make things right with both God and man:

> *But if we judged ourselves rightly, we should*
> *not be judged. But when we are judged, we*
> *are disciplined by the Lord in order that we*
> *may not be condemned along with the world*
> (I Corinthians 11:31,32 NAS).

The mistake we commonly make is that we do not *then* accept God's forgiveness. Oh, we cry out to Him for forgiveness, and God does in fact cleanse and forgive us of sin, but *we don't forgive ourselves.* We continue to blame ourselves and carry the burden of our guilt. Then we allow Satan to parade our past sins before us in an infinite loop. We become hostage to blame. Feeling defeated and utterly discouraged, we say to ourselves, "Well, I blew it again! I'm not very good at living this Christian life." Our self-esteem evaporates to the degree that we become impotent Christians, so discouraged that we fall away.

> *Let us draw near to God with a sincere heart*
> *in full assurance of faith, having our hearts*
> *sprinkled to **cleanse us from a guilty***
> ***conscience** and having our bodies washed*
> *with pure water* (Hebrews 10:22 NIV).

Guilt is a device that the enemy uses to neutralize Christians. Hebrews calls it "a guilty conscience." It is a life wrecker and a *faith killer.* A guilty conscience disables your faith. Faith is vitally important because it is the force that launches God's best—His will—into your life.

Faith is what allows you to be an "overcoming" Christian, doing exploits for God. Each of the spiritual heroes from Abel to the prophets did great things for God *by faith* (see Hebrews 11). God desires you to do great deeds, but how can you when your faith is held captive to blame? How can you believe God for *anything* if you are convinced that you are a "low-grade," "second-class," always inadequate Christian?

Doctrine of Defeat

Some have formulated blame into a doctrine of defeat. In their deception, they have named it "humility" and call it a virtue. Don't fall prey to this empty form of humility, by taking pride in humbleness. It will derail your faith and make you un-pleasing to God, because God cannot use faith-*less* people for His glory and their benefit:

> *But without faith it is impossible to please him: for he that cometh to God must believe that he is, and that he is a rewarder of them that diligently seek him* (Hebrews 11:6).

Jesus' shed blood has *made* you a son or daughter of the Most High God. God sees you as *righteous* through the eyes of grace: *"For He made Him who knew no sin to be sin for us, that we might become the righteousness of God in Him"* (II Corinthians 5:21 NKJ).

Stop blaming yourself! Start blaming the devil for the "dirty tricks" he has played on you! Repent for being deceived, and make a decision *now* to be what God has called you to be—a victorious Christian, a hero of faith, a world shaker, and a mountain mover. Step out of the crowd of "wannabes," shrug off the burden of guilt, and be *all* that you can be—in Him.

Trials, Temptations, and Adversities—Defined

A temptation or an adversity, the enduring of which proves the merit of an individual's faith. For the Christian, to encounter adversity is to undergo a trial in which his faith is proved either true or false before God, the highest judge. Since many positive things come about through such trials, Christians are urged to rejoice at their occurrence (James 1:2; I Peter 4:13). Christ Himself set the example in how trials should be endured when He defeated Satan's temptations by appealing to the word and will of God (Luke 4:1-13).

(Reprinted by permission from *Nelson's Illustrated Bible Dictionary* © 1986, Thomas Nelson Publishers)

The Comfort of Friends

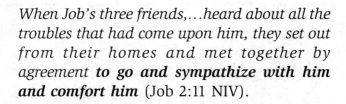

> *When Job's three friends,...heard about all the*
> *troubles that had come upon him, they set out*
> *from their homes and met together by*
> *agreement **to go and sympathize with him***
> ***and comfort him** (Job 2:11 NIV).*

Alone, Job sat—without his dearly loved children or
a sympathetic wife, and with none of the comforts that his
fortune could have purchased. *Alone* he waited for the
outcome of his ordeal. Imagine how his flickering hope must
have flared with expectation as his dearest friends arrived.
Hope must have flooded his heart as they joined him and
shared his grief:

> *When they saw him from a distance, they*
> *could hardly recognize him; they began to*
> *weep aloud, and they tore their robes and*
> *sprinkled dust on their heads. Then they sat*
> *on the ground with him for seven days and*
> *seven nights. No one said a word to him,*
> *because they saw how great his suffering was*
> *(Job 2:12,13 NIV).*

Job must have looked hideous for his best friends to
"hardly recognize him." The devastation of Job's body must
have been terrible, to cause these men to "weep aloud" and
tear their clothing at the sight of him. So shaken were they
by Job's physical loss, and so distressed by his obvious
suffering, that out of respect, they sank to the ground with

Job and sat for seven days in total silence.

Sometimes the best gift we can give to those who are suffering is our *silent* support. A friend of mine received word that her son had been missing from his apartment in another state for a week or more. The police, of course, suspected foul play. During the following months, when there was no word of her son's whereabouts, members of a small prayer group came to her home regularly. They were not there to cheer her up artificially or to tell her glibly to "trust in the Lord." They were there in silence to show their support and love in a way that showed they shared this mother's grief. Solomon said it best, *"To every thing there is a season,...a time to keep silence, and a time to speak;"* (Ecclesiastes 3:1,7).

If only Job's friends had held to their purpose, resisted Satan, and taken a stand with Job against evil, what a *different* story it could have been!

Gap-stander or Gap-finder?

> *So I sought for a man among them who would* **make a wall, and stand in the gap** *before Me on behalf of the land, that I should not destroy it; but I found no one* (Ezekiel 22:30 NKJ).

Because their intentions were good, we might surmise that God inspired the friends of Job to come and comfort him. They could have been a gift from God to sustain him during his trial. They certainly could have played an important part in delivering Job from his problems and thereby enjoyed a part in the "intended end" that God had for him. Job's friends were meant to build a wall of protection around Job and to stand in the gaps of that hedge.

Doesn't it seem coincidental that Job had been attacked in *three* areas of his life—possessions, family, and health—and there were *three* friends who came to comfort him? Each friend could have chosen an area of need, a gap in his hedge, and *stood in the gap* for that area of Job's life. There were also three rounds of debate, but what if there had been three rounds of *prayer* for Job instead? What a difference there might have been!

After sitting for seven days in sympathy for Job, these friends could have stood, offered sacrifices, and prayed great intercessory prayers for him. Unfortunately, they missed their chance to be a blessing to their friend— defending him from the enemy and becoming a part of his restoration. Instead, they became a curse to Job— criticizing him and causing him to stumble. They could have been three "gap-standers." Instead, they chose to be a trio of "gap-finders."

It is very tempting to be a gap-finder—to criticize and condemn. For some unholy reason, it makes us feel *superior* when we focus our judgmental attitude upon the faults and mistakes of others. With a counterfeit sorrowful expression, we nod our head wisely and say, "Yes, it's a pity—but he got what he deserved." What if *we* got what we deserved? What if God was a vindictive judge who rained down fire bolts at *our* every mistake? I doubt any of us would be living.

Happily, though, we serve a *merciful* God whose grace far exceeds our sins—a God Who said to the woman caught in adultery, *"...Neither do I condemn thee: go, and sin no more"* (John 8:11). This God of mercy has called *us* to extend grace, mercy, and forgiveness:

> *Judge not, and ye shall not be judged: condemn*
> *not, and ye shall not be condemned: forgive,*
> *and ye shall be forgiven:...* (Luke 6:37).

Rather than condemn, we must weave a hedge of protection around those suffering the attacks of the enemy— a wall built by prayers and faith-filled statements rooted in God's Word, and energized by our faith. Satan wants to break through our barrier—trials, troubles, and tribulations are Satan's devices to create a gap of vulnerability:

> *He who digs a pit will fall into it, and*
> *whoever breaks through a wall will be bitten*
> *by a serpent* (Ecclesiastes 10:8 NKJ).

If your hedge is strong, the devil may come *against* it, but he will not be able to come *through* it.

Jesus Says, "No!"

> *Now there were some present at that time*
> *who told Jesus about the Galileans whose*
> *blood Pilate had mixed with their sacrifices.*
> *Jesus answered, "Do you think that these*
> *Galileans were worse sinners than all the*
> *other Galileans because they suffered this*
> *way?* **I tell you, no!** *But unless you repent,*
> *you too will all perish. Or those eighteen who*
> *died when the tower in Siloam fell on them—*

THE RIGHT QUESTIONS

Job was questioned by God out of the whirlwind. Sometimes the most effective means of teaching is to ask questions. The Lord wanted Job to do some thinking for himself. These were not merely rhetorical questions to be brushed over lightly; each deserved serious consideration and contemplation. God directed Job's attention first to the humanly unexplainable wonders of His inanimate creation:

The foundations of the earth (38:4)
The seas (38:8)
The sunrise (38:12)
The springs in the sea (38:16)
The gates of death (38:17)
The breadth of the earth (38:18)
The source of light (38:19)
The treasures of snow (38:22)
The rain (38:26)
The ice (38:29)
The stars (38:31)
The clouds (38:34)

do you think they were more guilty than all the others living in Jerusalem? **I tell you, no!** *But unless you repent, you too will all perish"* (Luke 13:1-5 NIV).

Calamities happen. Once Jesus was asked by His disciples, "Why do bad things happen?" Two notable tragedies had recently occurred—Pilate, the Roman governor of Israel, had murdered a number of Jews as they were offering a sacrifice, and a tower had fallen, killing innocent people. The disciples wondered if God was punishing these people for their sins.

We could ask the same question about today's tragedies—like the Oklahoma City bombing or the Columbine High School shootings. Did the victims deserve to die? Was God punishing them?

Jesus answers these questions as He answered His disciples, with a single, unmistakable word, "No!" Jesus declares, "No, an automobile accident isn't God's judgment. No, a house fire is not God's punishment. No, a tornado, hurricane, forest fire, drought, mud slide, or snow storm isn't divine retribution." The calamities men call "acts of God" are NOT God's acts or judgments. The book of Revelation tells us that, at the end time, God *will* judge the earth and all of its people—but every catastrophic event is not punishment from God.

In His answer to the disciples' questions, Jesus was warning them, "Be prepared! Tragedy could strike *you* and your life could end in the blink of an eye; so, you need to be *spiritually* prepared. Get right with God, repent of your sins, and turn from a sinful life style."

To further explain "why bad things happen to good

people," Jesus also gave a parable:

> *...A man had a fig tree, planted in his vineyard, and he went to look for fruit on it, but did not find any. So he said to the man who took care of the vineyard, "For three years now I've been coming to look for fruit on this fig tree and haven't found any. Cut it down! Why should it use up the soil?" "Sir," the man replied, "leave it alone for one more year, and I'll dig around it and fertilize it. If it bears fruit next year, fine! If not, then cut it down"* (Luke 13:6-9 NIV).

The gardener in this parable represents an intercessor, asking God for a delay in sentencing—another chance for the unproductive tree. Millions of people in our world are like the unproductive fig tree. This story points out their need for an intercessor. Today, Jesus stands at the right hand of God, and Hebrews 7:25 says that *"...he ever liveth to make intercession for them."* He intercedes with God for us and for the lives of our unsaved loved ones. We too are called to be intercessors—gap-standers—for the people in our lives and for the unsaved of our world.

Wag the Dog

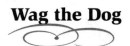

> *...much more those who receive the **abundance of grace** and of the gift of righteousness will reign in life through the One, Jesus Christ* (Romans 5:17 NAS).

"Abundance of grace" is a lifestyle. Grace does not come to us in dribbles and spurts based upon our merit, but is available in *abundance*. The dictionary defines *abundance* as "plentiful, lavish, overflowing." God has an overflowing amount of "grace" to meet your every need. Grace makes it possible for us to "reign" or prevail in all the situations of our life—even in our tests, trials, and tribulations.

Can a *victim* "reign in life"? One can't be a victim and a victor at the same time. We need to shed our victim mentality and stop believing that we are at the mercy of someone or something else—our past mistakes, a dysfunctional family history, the devil, life's circumstances, or other things. Victims accept bad things as their lot in life, but *you* do not have to settle for a life of defeat! God gave His son to die the death of the cross so that you could live in "abundance of grace"! He redeemed you to be a *conqueror for Christ*. Deuteronomy 28:13 says that you are the head and not the tail, above and not beneath. Even if you are presently at the tail-end of life, you can wag the dog!

God in the Context of the Impossible —El Shaddai

Grace is like a blank check drawn upon the Bank of Heaven. However, a check is only as good as the person who stands behind it. To know that our grace check will cash, we need to find out Who the signer of the check is and discover if His "grace" reserves are adequate to our needs. The signer on your grace check is El Shaddai.

Over the centuries, God has used various methods to

reveal Himself to mankind. In early times, even before Moses penned the first word of the Old Testament, God had begun to reveal Himself through His "names." (Of course, the Bible is where God is most clearly revealed.) In our culture, an individual's name can mean anything—or nothing—but in early times, names *defined* an individual. God used various names to describe Himself to ancient people.

In the Bible, there are some 20 names for God. Most people are familiar with the name *Jehovah,* which means "the revealing One" and refers to the intimate and very personal way God relates to us as a Father relates to His children.

Another name for God is *El Shaddai,* which means "He who is more than sufficient to meet your needs." Abraham was the first person to meet God as El Shaddai. (El Shaddai is the God of the impossible, God of all grace, God of all miracles, God of all supply.)

When Abraham was 99 years old and his wife was 89, God came to them in the *context of the impossible* and told them they were going to have a child. Even in ancient times, when people lived longer lives, 89 and 99 years of age were too old to have a child. The situation sounded impossible! In the natural, it *truly* was impossible; however, no situation is hopeless for El Shaddai! Within a year's time, baby Isaac was born to Abraham and Sarah.

The name *El Shaddai* is used 48 times in the book of Job. Why does God manifest Himself as El Shaddai in this book? Because God was saying, through every step of Job's trials—the loss of his fortune, his children, and his health—"I'm the God who can resolve your impossible situation. My grace is bigger than your loss. Your God is El Shaddai Who can meet *ALL* your needs."

El Shaddai is knocking upon *your* door. He stands waiting for you to get past *blame* and *guilt* and to call upon His grace. God is "waiting in the wings" to take center stage in the tragedies of your life.

> **The name El Shaddai is used 48 times in the book of Job.**

Battlefield Earth

One of the most important things we learn from Job's story is that we, like Job, are aware of only a very small portion of what is going on around us. We see only those things that occur in the *physical* world, and we are largely oblivious to what is happening in the *spiritual* world. We *hear* the bill collectors, *see* our loved ones die, *feel* the loss of a broken marriage, *taste* the agony of defeat—but we don't observe Satan behind the blackout curtain, like a puppet master, pulling the strings.

As people of the tangible world, we do not see the bright supernatural light that shines from the Cross, bathing us in hope, or the angels whom God has sent to "minister" to us. Neither do we see the sympathetic eyes of Jesus looking down upon us from the right hand of the Father where He intercedes on our behalf. No, like Job, all we see is "battlefield earth."

Trial By Debate

Job went through a trial of faith by *ordeal* when he lost his wealth, his children, and his health. The Bible says that Job did not sin during any of these troubles. Then his friends appeared and Job faced trials of a different sort—trial by *debate*. Remember that Satan's objective was to erode Job's character and get him to denounce God by making him question the *character* of God—God's goodness and grace—so that he would curse God.

Many of us, like Job, are better at dealing with tangible problems than with verbal attacks. Hidden, behind the scenes, Satan was crafting cleverly reasoned arguments to attack Job's core beliefs about God, and to fuel his faith in his own righteousness. Job's enemy was the same cruel monster who attacks us today. Satan still uses the same tactic—the words of men—to undermine our faith in a "good" God and our relationship with Him.

The most difficult verbal attacks to survive are those that come from other Christians. Make no mistake, Job's accusers were not heathens and villains, they were dear friends, people he loved and respected...yes, fellow believers.

On the eighth day of his friends' visit, Job opened his mouth and put his foot in it. No, he did not curse God—he cursed himself: *"... Job opened his mouth and cursed the day of his birth"* (Job 3:1 NIV). For the next 25 verses, Job laments the fact that he is alive. Job was a man overwhelmed by his circumstances, wishing he were dead.

God Crushes

Following Job's outburst, his oldest friend, Eliphaz (*Eliphaz* means "God crushes"), stood and, instead of supporting and standing in the gap for Job, began to question, rebuke, and accuse him of sinning. Poor Job must have been shocked! His friends had been supportive up until this moment. Perhaps he paused his endless scratching to stare in surprise at the unexpected accusations of his friend, Eliphaz.

Apparently during the seven days of silence, Eliphaz had come to some false conclusions concerning Job's plight. Eliphaz argued that the only *possible* reason for Job's dilemma was sin—somehow, some way, Job had grievously sinned and was now suffering God's punishment. Eliphaz used psychology mixed with religion and mysticism to attack Job.

The basis for Eliphaz's criticism of Job was flawed. The Bible tells the stories of many innocent people whose suffering was unrelated to sin. David, although innocent, suffered for many years at the hand of Saul. The prophet Jeremiah was thrown into a dungeon for preaching God's Word. Jesus was persecuted and crucified, yet He was totally innocent of sin.

At first, Eliphaz complimented Job. Job probably nodded in agreement, mentally saying, "Yes, that's right" when Eliphaz said:

> *Think how you have instructed many, how you have strengthened feeble hands. Your words have supported those who stumbled; you have strengthened faltering knees* (Job 4:3,4 NIV).

Once he had gained Job's confidence and established credibility through his compliments, Eliphaz "nailed" Job with, *"...those who plow evil and those who sow trouble reap it"* (Job 4:8 NIV). He was stating that Job was reaping trouble because of his sins.

During his attack upon Job, Eliphaz used expressions that were the oral version of truths that we accept today. Many of his sayings, and the statements of the other friends, are found elsewhere in God's Word. One example is:

> *Blessed is the man whom God corrects; so do not despise the discipline of the Almighty* (Job 5:17 NIV).

Satan knows the Bible better than most Christians do and will twist a passage of Scripture to attack a believer.

To add further weight to his accusation, Eliphaz claimed to have received spiritual guidance through a vision:

> *Fear came upon me, and trembling, which made all my bones shake. Then a spirit passed before my face; the hair on my body stood up. It stood still, but I could not discern its appearance. A form was before my eyes; there was silence; then I heard a voice saying: Can a mortal be more righteous than God? Can a man be more pure than his Maker?...* (Job 4:14-17 NKJ).

What an eerie vision! It sounds haunting. From our perspective, we know that this vision did not come from God. This could have been the device Satan used to turn

The Mysteries

"When you're through thinking about those mysteries," God said to Job, "here are a few more wonders for you to contemplate in the animal kingdom":

The lion (38:39)
The raven (38:41)
The wild goats (39:1)
The wild ass (39:5)
The unicorn (39:9)
The peacocks (39:13)
The ostrich (39:13)
The horse (39:19)
The hawk (39:26)
The eagle (39:27)
The behemoth (40:15)
The leviathan (41:1)

What do you suppose God was getting at in asking all those questions? I think He was saying, "Job, when you understand the mysteries surrounding all these things, then maybe you will begin to understand the higher mysteries of My dealings with man. But until then— TRUST ME!"

Eliphaz from a "comforter" into an "accuser." Regardless of whether it was caused by too much spicy pizza or by Satan, a personal vision was hard for Job to refute. We, too, need to be cautious of the visions and "words from God" that we receive from others.

Some years ago when my husband, Wally, and I were planning a trip to Texas, a lady who attended our church warned me that she had dreamed that if we drove to Texas we would be killed in an automobile accident. Naturally, I was quite upset and told Wally what she had said. His reply was, "I don't feel any check in my spirit about going to Texas. If God wants to give us a warning, He can speak just as easily to you and me as to that lady." We went ahead and drove to Texas. Nothing happened; we didn't even have a close call. Sometimes sincere people are merely misled, but there are also people whose motives are selfish, self-seeking, or just plain evil. That is why the Bible says,

> *Beloved, do not believe every spirit, but test the spirits, whether they are of God;...*
> (I John 4:1 NKJ).

Sharp Nail

It's not an accident that the name of Job's next "friend" was *Bildad,* which means "sharp nail." The devil wants to nail you. He will use people to hurl sharp, cruel, painful digs at you. Bildad based his arguments upon "tradition." He tried to use the yardstick of history and former ages to prove his arguments.

Bildad attacked Job using a weapon sure to bring

anguish—the death of his children. Pouring salt in the wound of Job's loss, Bildad claimed that Job's children died because they had sinned against God. You will recall that Job offered a sacrifice for each of his children every seven days just to ensure that any sin they *might* have committed was covered by the blood. So in effect, Bildad was saying to Job, "Your prayers for your children were for nothing. God didn't even hear them."

This is an argument Satan often uses against us. He whispers, "You are so insignificant and sinful that God won't answer your prayers. He doesn't even pay attention to them." During a trial, or when we have prayed a long time for something dear to our hearts, we are especially susceptible to this strategy of the enemy.

Bildad said:

Ask the former generations and find out what their fathers learned,...Will they not instruct you and tell you? Will they not bring forth words from their understanding? (Job 8:8,10 NIV).

"Look back to tradition to find your answers," is what Bildad was saying to Job. Tradition is like an ancient Egyptian mummy: it has the form of truth, but the spirit that gives it life is long since gone. It is empty and dead. Relying on tradition for all the answers is a mistake that some church groups and Christians make, and it keeps them from participating in the *fresh* things that God is doing in our day.

When Wally and I were first starting our church, a growth began to develop under one of my fingernails. It was *really* ugly and it got bigger and bigger and began to push the nail out. I rebuked it in Jesus' name and cursed it to die, but it did not get better right away. One of the women who attended our little church noticed it and said, "What is that ugly looking thing? That looks malignant." I told her it was cursed and drying up. Her reply was, "I had a friend with a growth just like that—and she died." That was *tradition* talking. Who do you suppose inspired the woman to tell me the growth was cancerous and would kill me? The same being who inspired Bildad's traditional attack upon Job—Satan.

Traditionalists will remind us that "God is the same, yesterday, today, and forever." Indeed He does not change; however, His methods of dealing with men have always been contemporary to the culture and the times. We cannot restrict God by expecting Him to do things in the same way as He has done in the past. Neither does God restrict Himself to His past methods.

Chatter Box

Eliphaz *hinted* that Job was a great sinner. Bildad *suggested* that Job's sin was a family affair, resulting in the death of his children. Zophar, the third "friend" to confront Job, went even further: he *charged* Job openly with sin. *Zophar,* whose name means "chatterer," used "common sense" to blame Job's trials on his great sinfulness. Zophar had the audacity to say, *"...Know therefore that God exacts from you less than your iniquity deserves"* (Job 11:6 NKJ). He was saying that Job got a great bargain from God and that, in fact, he deserved a far greater punishment.

Zophar was a talker—talk, talk, talk. He was probably

one of those people who constantly interrupts others and gives all the answers before even studying the situation.

Job's "counselors" argued from personal experience, tradition, and common sense. Job did not need this kind of advice; he needed the *truth* from God's Word, and so do you and I. Instead of going to *human* sources for wisdom, we need the *real* thing—wisdom from God's Word.

Mr. Humble's Reply

Job's response to his friends was full of self-righteousness, self-pity, anger, snide remarks, and, occasionally, wisdom with intermittent flashes of spiritual insight. During the course of his defense, Job spoke the personal pronouns, "I," "me," or "my," thousands of times. Does that seem excessive to you? You might ask, "Is this the man whom God called *"perfect"*? God was speaking by grace and calling *"...those things which be not as though they were"* (Romans 4:17). When you blow it as Job did, God isn't critical; He speaks of *you* through grace.

Although Job knew that he was devout and had kept God's laws, he also knew that he could not claim sinless perfection before God. Job realized that no matter how much he *did* to be righteous, it could never be enough. It is the same for us. Job recognized that he needed a Savior. Although this realization may be familiar to you, it was a most uncommon thought in ancient times.

Job saw that regardless of how much we *do,* and irrespective of how hard we *try,* our "good works" cannot build a bridge across the chasm of sin that separates us from a sinless God. The bridge, salvation from sin and death, had to come from God's side. Ultimately, Jesus became our bridge:

> *Being justified freely by His grace through the redemption that is in Christ Jesus,...For the law of the Spirit of life in Christ Jesus has made me free from the law of sin and death. For* **what the law could not do in that it was weak through the flesh, God did by sending His own Son in the likeness of sinful flesh,** *on account of sin: He condemned sin in the flesh* (Romans 3:24; 8:2,3 NKJ).

Job hit upon another important truth—man's inability to represent himself before God without a mediator:

> *For He is not a man, as I am, that I may answer Him, and that we should go to court together. Nor is there any mediator between us, who may lay his hand on us both* (Job 9:32,33 NKJ).

Paul, in the New Testament, tells us Who our mediator is: *"For there is one God and one Mediator between God and men, the Man Christ Jesus,"* (I Timothy 2:5 NKJ).

Unfortunately, Job knew nothing of an advocate or attorney named Jesus, or of the Holy Spirit. What about you? When you are faced with a crisis, do you search for an advocate to plead your case? Do you have the assurance of the Comforter within, and the sure knowledge that Jesus is your advocate at the right hand of God the Father in heaven?

Several years ago, a friend of mine (a Christian

woman I will call Ellen) received a flu shot. There were rumors of bad side effects following the shot, but it was not until three months later that Ellen suddenly found it hard to move her arms and legs. One day, while driving, she had the terrifying experience of totally losing her vision.

Ellen spent the next three months sleeping 20 hours a day! During this time, her friends and neighbors took turns cooking meals for her family, looking after her two young children, and caring for her home. She was diagnosed with Guillain-Barre syndrome, which threatened to cause paralysis to the lungs and other vital organs. The situation was desperate!

However, Ellen and her husband *knew* they had a Mediator and Comforter; and they began to pray and draw closer to the Lord. "God became more real to me, and I truly learned to give Him my cares since I couldn't do anything at all," Ellen told me later.

After six months, Ellen began to function reasonably well, but it was eight years before she was totally restored. Because of her infirmity, she found it exhausting to do even the easiest tasks, and she would pray, "Lord, I need a parking space close to the door today" and "Lord, I'm so weary. Please, no line at the checkout counter or stoplights on the way home." With a smile, Ellen reports, "I'm not exaggerating when I say that every request was met, and I mean *every* one."

Through her experience, Ellen learned that, although the days were difficult, she was never alone: the Holy Spirit, her Comforter, was always near to help, and Christ, her Mediator, would see her through. When unexplained trials enter your life, instead of asking, "Why is this happening to me!" just remember you have a Mediator and Comforter to see you through the suffering to the blessing that waits on the other side.

Devil-Defeating Words

Job hoped for an end to his trials. On some days, he even hoped for death as an end. However, during his better moments, Job longed for God to save him from his trials and exonerate him before his friends. Although Job barely had a clue who was persecuting him, he said something that that was a "back-breaker" to Satan: *"Though He slay me, yet will I trust Him...."* (Job 13:15 NKJ).

Remember that the primary goal of Satan during any trial is the same for you as it was for Job—to alienate you from God. The resolve that will defeat Satan and bring you through your trial is the steadfast determination that God is good. He wants only your best, and you can entrust Him with your very life. However, to make this a strong conviction, you must start by trusting God during your trials.

The second power statement that will defeat the devil is found in Job 19:25-27:

> *For I know that my Redeemer lives, and He shall stand at last on the earth; And after my skin is destroyed, this I know, that in my flesh I shall see God, Whom I shall see for myself, and my eyes shall behold, and not another. How my heart yearns within me!* (NKJ).

This is a declaration of your belief in Christ as your Redeemer. You are saying that you believe that Jesus was the Son of God, lived a sinless life on this earth, and offered Himself up to God as a sacrificial offering for *your* sins. You must have a certainty that *your* sins are forgiven and that Jesus is not only the Savior of the world, but also *your* personal Redeemer.

Lastly, Satan would like you to believe that he is all-powerful, and that you are at his mercy. He wants you to think that he is even greater than God, and that your problems are too big for God to meet. Consequently, you need to declare with Job:

> *I know that* **You** **[God]** ***can do everything,*** *and that no purpose of Yours can be withheld from You* (Job 42:2 NKJ).

Another **Friend?**

Four men came to comfort Job in his time of trouble. The fourth friend, Elihu, was so junior in age and status to the other men that his name isn't even mentioned until the 32nd chapter of Job. The first three friends, rather than being comforters, turned out to be "discomforters"— gap finders who falsely accused Job and his children of every sort of sin. The fourth friend, "Elihu," which means *my God is He*, was a *gap-stander*. He came to Job not as a judge but as a brother.

At this point, if you were hearing the story of Job for the first time, you might feel that *someone* needed to come on the scene to set things right. God is that "someone." Elihu, however, was the human bridge which served to prepare Job for God's arrival.

After the others had finally given up berating Job, and Job had finished justifying himself, Elihu was so upset with both Job and his friends that he could no longer remain silent:

> *Then was kindled the wrath of Elihu the son of Barachel the Buzite, of the kindred of Ram: against Job was his wrath kindled, because he justified himself rather than God. Also against his three friends was his wrath kindled, because they had found no answer, and yet had condemned Job* (Job 32:2,3).

After listening to Job's utterings, Elihu knew that Job's biggest problem was that he no longer believed in the goodness of God. He told Job, "You complain about not hearing from God; stop *fighting* God so that He *can* speak to you."

> *For God may speak in one way, or in another, yet man does not perceive it. In a dream, in a vision of the night, when deep sleep falls upon men, while slumbering on their beds, Then He opens the ears of men, and seals their instruction* (Job 33:14-16 NKJ).

God wants to instruct *you* in the midst of *your* trial. He wants to give you guidance that will deliver you from your situation. If, like Job, your relationship with God is poor, you won't be able to hear God's voice.

To further prepare Job for God's arrival, Elihu pointed out Job's sin—accusing God of being unjust:

> *But you have said in my hearing—I heard the very words—"I am pure and without sin; I am clean and free from guilt. Yet God has found fault with me; he considers me his enemy." But I tell you, **in this you are not right**, for God is greater than man. **It is unthinkable that God would do wrong,** that the Almighty would pervert justice* (Job 33:8-10,12 NIV).

That is the bottom line to every problem, crisis, and difficulty: *"It is unthinkable that God would do wrong."* Job compounded his problems by putting himself out of touch with God through his sin. Job effectively cut *himself* off from God's help during his trials.

Not "Why, Lord?" but, "What, Lord?"

Early in this chapter, we noticed that during Job's trials Satan disappeared from the stage and worked behind the scenes. God also became invisible during the unfolding drama. Just as Satan didn't stop stalking Job, God didn't stop trying to help him. Not only did God send the comforters, whom Satan perverted into tormentors, but God tried to maintain contact with Job "through it all" in order to comfort and guide him.

When you are in the midst of a problem, God is reaching out to *you*. He may send people to help, counsel, and comfort; He might instruct you in a vision or dream; He will most certainly speak to you through His Word and through anointed ministries. However, you must be receptive. Don't cut off communications by blaming God for your trials, by rebuffing people who try to help, or by ceasing to read the Word. You must be discriminating, though. Satan can send people to influence you as well.

> *The Almighty is beyond our reach and exalted in power; in his justice and great righteousness, **he does not oppress*** (Job 37:23 NIV).

The Rescue Mission

Elihu had turned Job's heart from self-pity, self-centeredness, and a corrupted defense of his righteousness, so that Job was finally ready to hear God's voice—and God was ready to speak. You, too, need to get ready—because when God Almighty speaks, things are created, lives are transformed, and the works of the enemy are destroyed.

In an era when mechanical force was unknown and electrical and atomic energy untapped, God arrived in the most majestic, powerful, and forceful way people could understand—in a whirlwind. *Whirlwind* means "hurricane, storm, tempest" and comes from a root word that means "to rush upon." The Lord was *rushing upon* Job with words that would turn his *captivity* into *liberty.*

When Jesus came to earth, He had the same mission:

> *The Spirit of the Lord is upon Me, because He has anointed Me to preach the gospel to the poor; he has sent Me to heal the brokenhearted, **to proclaim liberty to the captives** and recovery of sight to the blind, **to set at liberty those who are oppressed;*** (Luke 4:18 NKJ).

Goodness that Leads to Repentance

How did God restore Job? Did He say, "Job I'm so weary of your talk, talk, talk that I'm here to shut you up?" Or, "You're disgusting to me; I'm disappointed in you. At the beginning, I told the devil that you were 'perfect' and look what you did; you blamed your problems on me! You deserve your fate, so go ahead, give up and die." No, God did not blast Job; He "reasoned" with him.

That is the way God restores people who are in trouble. He doesn't discharge a thunderbolt at them. God says:

> ***"Come now, and let us reason together,"*** *says the LORD, "Though your sins are like scarlet, they shall be as white as snow; though they are red like crimson, they shall be as wool. If you are willing and obedient, you shall eat the good of the land;* (Isaiah 1:18,19 NKJ).

God began to question Job. In fact, He bombarded him with 85 questions at one time! God used this same method of "question and answer" to restore Jonah. Perhaps you recall that after Jonah had been swallowed by the fish and had *finally* submitted to God's will by preaching to the wicked people of Nineveh, he sat under the little gourd tree pouting, in total depression waiting to die.

What was Jonah's problem? All the people of Nineveh were saved, and the city had avoided destruction. So why was he upset? In spite of Jonah's ridiculous position, God did not deal harshly with him. Instead, God said, "Do you have a reason to be angry? Shouldn't I have saved all those thousands of people and animals?" Just as God let Jonah *see for himself* the truth, so He led Job to the truth. He restored Jonah and Job by reasoning with them through questions and answers.

Are You a *"Gever"* or an *"Enosh"*?

> *Now prepare yourself like a man* [enosh]; *I will question you, and you shall answer Me* (Job 38:3 NKJ).

Was God telling Job to "be a man?—be macho," or "stand at attention, suck in your stomach, push your chest out, and look straight ahead while I really let you have it"? No, God was saying something totally different.

The Hebrew language contains four different words for the English word "man." *Adam* is the first, and it literally means "earthy, made out of earth." Another word for man is *ish,* which means "a man who wants a reciprocal relationship." For example, Adam, in his role as Eve's husband was *ish* and Eve as his wife was *ishi.* The third word for man is *enosh,* which means "weak, sickly, and sinful." This word for man is first used in Genesis where it says, "*...then began* [enosh] *men to call upon the name of the*

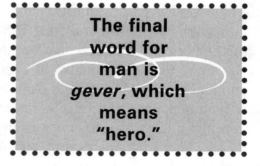
The final word for man is *gever,* which means "hero."

LORD" (4:26 KJV). It is used when a man recognizes his sinfulness and need for God. God was saying, "Job I want to talk to you like a man who recognizes his need for God's help." The final word for man is *gever,* which means "hero."

In the beginning of the story, when God spoke of Job, He used the word *gever.*

> *...Have you considered My servant Job, that there is none like him on the earth, a blameless and upright man [gever or hero], one who fears God and shuns evil?* (Job 1:8 NKJ).

Now, nine months, 37 chapters, many disasters and trials later, Job must humble himself and recognize that he has slipped. He must come out of denial, disavow his self-righteousness and pride, and declare, "I am a needy man, an *enosh."* The attitude of the enosh is the starting point for anyone who wants God to intervene in their crises.

God wants each of us to be a *gever*—a hero, an upright person who fears God and shuns evil. Practically every time the word *gever* appears in the Old Testament, along with it is found the word "trust." The Bible says, *"Blessed is the man [gever] who makes the LORD his trust,...* (Psalms 40:4 NIV). What did Job need to do and what do *we* need to do to change from an *enosh* to a *gever?* From a victim to a victor? From overwhelmed to an overcomer? We need to learn to *trust* in the Lord. God makes you a promise that when you trust in Him, He will direct you through every situation of your life:

> *Trust in the LORD with all your heart, and*

lean not on your own understanding; In all your ways acknowledge Him, and He shall direct your paths (Proverbs 3:5,6 NKJ).

Return to Jehovah

In the first two chapters of Job, God called himself *Jehovah*, and Jehovah is the intimate word for God. When God is talking about an intimate personal relationship with man, He uses the word *Jehovah*. During Job's trials, we learned that the name used for God is *El Shaddai*—the Almighty One, All Sufficient One. At that time, God was saying to Job, I am enough to meet all your needs. However, in these final chapters, the word God uses for Himself is, again, *Jehovah*. God is reminding Job of his need to return to an intimate relationship with Him.

By calling Himself Jehovah, God is saying, "I want to know you. Could we have a little talk? Could I be kind to you today? Would you like to give me all your cares and worries? Could I tell you how much I love you? I love you so much that I sent My Son to die for you."

Most people respond to that measure of love from God by saying, "I'm unworthy, and sinful, I can't receive that kind of love." However, God says, "I see you as 'perfect' through the eyes of grace, and you appear as a son or daughter whom I deeply love." *This is your moment, don't allow your feelings of unworthiness generated by self-blame or anything else to keep you from sweet intimacy with God.* God knows you aren't "perfect" but He knows that you are *maturing*. (You are better than you used to be.) Through your trust in Him, with His help and by His grace, you are becoming a *gever*—a hero, the very person God has called you to be.

We need to learn from the negative side of Job. People may begin to talk against God to *you*, too. They might try to trick you through legalism, saying you need to do this or do that. Someone may make sharp, barbed comments to you, and others may chatter so much that they distract you from your relationship with God. The enemy may whisper disturbing things in your ears. You can became so busy defending yourself that you, like Job, *lose* your relationship and intimacy with God.

> *...Therefore I have uttered what I did not understand, things too wonderful for me, which I did not know.* **I have heard of You by the hearing of the ear, but now my eye sees You.** *Therefore I abhor myself, and repent in dust and ashes* (Job 42:3,5,6 NKJ).

In Philippians 3:10, Paul says, *"That I may know him* [God]...." No one went through more trials and tribulations than Paul did, yet he was able to endure them all because of his intimate relationship with God. He learned how to handle trials so well that he was able to say, *"...we also glory in tribulations..."* (Romans 5:3 NKJ).

Grace or Dis-grace

> *After the LORD had said these things to Job, he said to Eliphaz the Temanite, "I am angry with you and your two friends, because* **you have not spoken of me what is right, as my servant Job has.** *So now take seven bulls and*

> *seven rams and go to my servant Job and sacrifice a burnt offering for yourselves. **My servant Job will pray for you, and I will accept his prayer** and not deal with you according to your folly..."* (Job 42:7,8 NIV).

Though angry at the other three friends, God did not say that He was angry with Elihu. Elihu was God's bridge, the only person who stood in the gap for Job. However, did you notice what God said about Job himself? First, God *again* called Job, "My Servant" as he had at first. Then, He told Job's tormentors, "You said wrong things about me, but Job said righteous things." Wait a minute! We've already seen that Job said "wrong things" too! Is Job God's pet? No, Job is God's *repenter*. Is God forgetful? Yes, God buries our *forgiven* sins in the "sea of forgetfulness." Once Job repented of speaking wrongful things, God literally "forgot" they had ever been said!

Job wasted a lot of energy and breath trying to vindicate himself with his friends. He couldn't change the mind of even one of them. However, God vindicated Job with a single sentence. You will never convince your critics that you are right and, like Job, you can waste a lot of time and energy trying. Allow God to vindicate you.

God's Pattern for Blessing

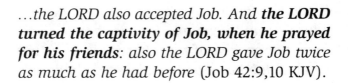

> *...the LORD also accepted Job. And **the LORD turned the captivity of Job, when he prayed for his friends**: also the LORD gave Job twice as much as he had before* (Job 42:9,10 KJV).

First, Job's relationship with God was restored when he repented after God talked to him. Job renewed his intimacy with God. However, nothing else had changed in Job's life—he still had painful boils from head to toe, his family was still gone, and he was still financially devastated. You should notice that God did not automatically bless Job when he reestablished relationship with Him. Prosperity is not an *automatic* result of salvation or recommitment to Christ—something more is required.

God required Eliphaz and the other two friends to offer blood sacrifices for their sins, but even that was not enough to restore *their* relationship with Him. God also required Job to pray (intercede) for them. What is happening here? For nine of the longest months of Job's life these men had rebuked, chastised, slandered, and denounced him—and Job had in turn said some pretty harsh things against them, too. Job's three *best* friends had become his *worst* enemies.

Job could have thought, "These guys have unfairly punished me for nine months. If I withhold my prayer for them, God will give them what they deserve." The friends could have countered with, "I don't care if God *did* forgive him—what about the ugly things Job said about *me*?" In order for Job to intercede for his friends, they had to reconcile and forgive one another. Job and his friends were obedient: they reconciled, and he prayed for them.

God may also require you to clean up the mess of your situations. Until you take this often-difficult step, you are *stuck* in the middle of God's process for blessing. God may require you to *make things right* with a person. That could mean many things. Whatever it is *you* must do—do it so that you can get on with God's process of blessing.

Types of Suffering	Correct Response	"Grace" Benefits
Circumstances (Weather conditions; repressive civil laws; "accidents"; sickness)	Focus on Jesus (Matthew 6:22) Rest in the Lord (Psalms 37:7)	Peace of God (Isaiah 26:3) Contentment (Philippians 4:11)
Sin (Personal wrongdoing)	Repent! Confess (I John 1:9)	Favor (Proverbs 13:15) Cleansing (I John 1:9)
Satan (Paul's thorn) (II Corinthians 12)	Submit to God Resist the devil (James 4:7) Blood & the Word (Revelation 12:11)	Victory over evil Overcomer (Revelation 2:26, Revelation 12:11)
Relationships (wife/husband; employee/employer; parent/child)	Unconditional love (Ephesians 5:25) Pray for wisdom (James 1:5) Forgiveness (Ephesians 4:32)	Harmony at home (Psalms 133:1) Favor at work (Proverbs 8:35) Honor (Proverbs 11:16)
Righteousness (Persecution on the job, by the government, by a spouse, by unsaved people)	Forgiveness (Ephesians 4:32) Pray for enemies (Luke 6:28) Do good (Luke 6:27) Bless enemies (I Peter 3:9) Share the gospel (I Peter 4:4-6) Glorify God (I Peter 4:16) Use soft words (Proverbs 15:1)	Happiness (I Peter 4:14) Spirit of glory rests on you (I Peter 4:14) Rejoicing at Jesus' return (I Peter 4:13)

You may need to forgive those who have wounded you. Regardless of whether the other person is sorry or cares that they've hurt you, you must by God's grace forgive them. Forgiveness is not a feeling or emotion; it is a reasoned act. Sometimes you must disregard your feelings and make a spiritual determination to say, "God, by *your* power working in me, I forgive. Heal my wounded heart and take away my bitterness."

Once Job had shown his obedience by praying for his friends, he opened the way for God to bless him, and the Bible says, *"And the LORD turned the captivity of Job..."* (Job 42:10). The "process of blessing" was complete, and what a *blessing* he received!

Above and Beyond

*Now to Him who is able to do **exceedingly abundantly above all that we ask or think**, according to the power that works in us,* (Ephesians 3:20 NKJ).

Job would have been grateful just to be free of pain and allowed to return to his simple, quiet life surrounded by friends and family. He would have been satisfied with just enough prosperity to live normally. Job would have been delighted if God had given him an *adopted* son to cherish and carry on his name. However, God had much bigger plans and much grander things for Job. Likewise, God's plans for *you* far exceed what you could "ask or think."

*...the LORD gave Job **twice as much as he***

*had before. Then came there unto him all his brethren, and all his sisters, and all they that had been of his acquaintance before, and did eat bread with him in his house:...every man also gave him a piece of money, and every one an earring of gold. So **the LORD blessed the latter end of Job more than his beginning**: for he had fourteen thousand sheep, and six thousand camels, and a thousand yoke of oxen, and a thousand she asses. **He had also seven sons and three daughters.** After this lived Job an hundred and forty years, and saw his sons, and his sons' sons, even four generations. So Job died, being old and full of days* (Job 42:10-13,16,17).

God not only restored to Job double what had been taken by Satan, but assigned him a ministry—intercession. Job realized God's "intended end."

Can you imagine how Job's faith must have grown from his experience? How his compassion for the sick, despised, and disadvantaged multiplied? Now within Job beat the compassionate *heart of an intercessor.* What a blessing this powerful prayer warrior must have been to his family and those around him for the remainder of his long life! The evidence of Job's stature as an intercessor is his mention in the intercessors' "hall of fame" in Ezekiel 14:14:

"Even if these three men, Noah, Daniel, and Job, were in it, they would deliver only

Marilyn Hickey Ministries

Marilyn was a public school teacher when she met Wallace Hickey. After their marriage, Wally was called to the ministry and Marilyn began teaching home Bible studies.

The vision of Marilyn Hickey Ministries is to "cover the earth with the Word" (Isaiah 11:9). For more than 30 years, Marilyn Hickey has dedicated herself to an anointed, unique, and distinguished ministry of reaching out to people—from all walks of life—who are hungry for God's Word and all that He has for them. Millions have witnessed and acclaimed the positive, personal impact she brings through fresh revelation knowledge that God has given her through His Word.

Marilyn and Wally adopted their son Michael. Then through a fulfilled prophecy they had their daughter Sarah who, with her husband Reece Bowling, is now part of the ministry.

Marilyn has been the invited guest of government leaders and heads of state from many nations of the world. She is considered by many to be one of today's greatest ambassadors of God's Good News to this dark and hurting generation. The more Marilyn follows God's will for her life, the more God uses her to bring refreshing, renewal, and revival to the Body of Christ throughout the world. As His obedient servant, Marilyn desires to follow Him all the days of her life.

Marilyn founded her ministry "Life for Laymen" so that she could reach more people with her gift for practical Bible application.

Marilyn taught at Denver's "Happy Church"—now Orchard Road Christian Center (ORCC)—and hosted ministry conferences with husband Wally, pastor of ORCC.

At a retreat in 1976, Marilyn realized she was called to "cover the earth with the Word."

The ministry staff in the early days helped Marilyn answer the mail that came in response to her first 15-minute radio show.

Soon Marilyn realized she could reach more people through television. She and Wally hosted many well-known guests.

In Guatemala with former President Ephraim Rios-Mott

Marilyn has been the invited guest of government leaders and heads of state from many nations of the world.

In Egypt with Mrs. Anwar Sadat

In Venezuela with former first lady Mrs. Perez

Marilyn ministered to guerillas in Honduras and brought food and clothing to the wives and children who were encamped with their husbands.

The popular Bible-reading plan, *Time With Him,* began in 1978 and invited people to "read through the Bible with Marilyn." The monthly ministry magazine has since been renamed *Outpouring.* It now includes a calendar of ministry events, timely articles, and featured product offers.

Through Word to the World College
(formerly Marilyn Hickey Bible College),
Marilyn is helping to equip men
and women to take the gospel
around the world.

Sarah Bowling taught at Riverview
Christian Academy for several
years before her marriage, wrote
correspondence courses for the
Bible college…and has since joined
the ministry full-time where she
combines teaching at WWC with
ministry trips and Crusades.

God opened doors for the
supplying of Bibles to many
foreign lands—China, Israel,
Poland, Ethiopia, Russia,
Romania, and the Ukraine,
just to name a few.

The only woman on the board of directors of Dr. Cho's Church Growth International in Korea, Marilyn has spoken at his church many times and has also been a featured speaker at the Church Growth Conference held in Japan.

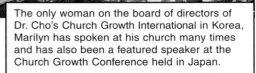

An international satellite broadcast was simulcast live from Israel to U.S. cities.

Marilyn made a series of trips to African refugee camps, supplying food for feeding programs and Bibles for the famine- and war-stricken communities.

Sarah began traveling overseas with her parents at an early age and developed a heart for missions.

Both Marilyn and Sarah have a strong heart for China, and have distributed thousands of Bibles and tracts there and in Russia.

The ministry expanded from its beginnings in a cardboard box of files on a kitchen table, to its first International Ministry Center built in 1985, to its present headquarters located in Greenwood Village, Colorado.

FILL THE SHIP, a special project of the Marilyn Hickey Children's Fund, supplies food and Bibles to various Third World countries, such as Haiti, the Philippines, Ethiopia, Honduras, and El Salvador.

The prime time television special, "A Cry for Miracles," featured co-host Gavin MacLeod.

Marilyn has been a guest several times on the 700 Club with host Pat Robertson.

Marilyn ministered in underground churches in Romania before any of the European communist countries were officially open.

Marilyn Hickey's Prayer Center handles calls from all over the U.S.— ministering to those who need agreement in prayer.

More than 1,500 ministry products help people in all areas of their life.

Marilyn received her honorary doctorate from Oral Roberts University. She now serves as the chairman of the Board of Regents.

Sarah graduated from ORU, and later earned her master's degree in History.

Marilyn and her Faith Covenant Partners respond to countless needs across the world. . .the devastating earthquakes in Mexico City, Romanian orphans, leprosy victims in Africa, orphans in war-torn Rwanda, street children in Brazil. . . all are touched by God's power.

MHM supports Mission of Mercy in Calcutta, headed by Huldah Buntain. Marilyn has made several trips there.

Airlift Manila provided much-needed food, Bibles, and personal supplies to the Philippines; MHM also raised funds to aid in the digging of water wells for those without clean drinking water.

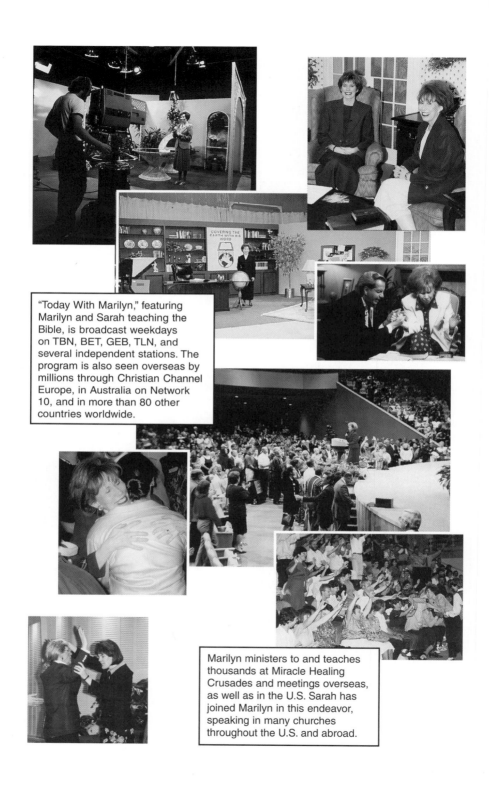

"Today With Marilyn," featuring Marilyn and Sarah teaching the Bible, is broadcast weekdays on TBN, BET, GEB, TLN, and several independent stations. The program is also seen overseas by millions through Christian Channel Europe, in Australia on Network 10, and in more than 80 other countries worldwide.

Marilyn ministers to and teaches thousands at Miracle Healing Crusades and meetings overseas, as well as in the U.S. Sarah has joined Marilyn in this endeavor, speaking in many churches throughout the U.S. and abroad.

Exciting ministry opportunities awaited Marilyn, Sarah, and their team of travelers in the Ukraine and Russia, as the doors opened for the Gospel.

Victim of the nuclear power plant disaster in Chernobyl

Marilyn has held Bible Encounters in Malaysia and Singapore. While traveling through Hong Kong she ministered to Vietnamese in a refugee camp.

National Women's Conferences and Pastors' Wives' Conventions were held across the U.S., exhorting women to "Change Their World!"

"Mastering Your Ministry: A Women's Mentoring Clinic" is Marilyn's new concept for providing in-depth teaching and personal ministry in an intimate setting.

The New York area Crusade hosted well-known national ministers and ministered to thousands at the Meadowlands Arena in New Jersey.

Ministry trips and cruises to places such as China, Indonesia, Russia, Greece, the Ukraine, Turkey, Africa, and Israel offer short-term missions' opportunities to travel to exotic places and minister with Marilyn and Sarah.

MHM now operates offices in several countries. Marilyn and Sarah also host yearly meetings, Crusades, and missions' projects in those countries.

Crowds of up to 200,000 attended the open-air Crusade in Bangalore, India.

In Islamabad, Pakistan, Marilyn held Ministry Training Schools. Total Crusade attendance was estimated at 70,000. Recent meetings in Karachi were estimated at 100,000!

Ministry Training Schools are held in many Third World countries, such as Sudan and Tanzania, and provide training and native language literature for local pastors and church leaders. Nightly Crusades are held to minister to the local populations.

themselves by their righteousness," says the Lord GOD (NKJ).

When Job finally got past blaming God, others, and himself, God turned things around and doubled the blessing on Job's life. God will do the same thing for you! He will take your trials and make them triumphs–your scars and make them stars to shine for your benefit and His glory.

It's really, really true. You *can* "bounce back from your setback" with a *double*-portion blessing!

The 5 Best Ways To...
Stop Blaming Yourself: "How Could I Have Been So Stupid?"

1. Don't believe the devil's lie that God causes sickness or crisis; read and meditate upon Psalms 103:2-5.

2. It's okay to give up a guilty conscience! Find out why in Hebrews 9:14.

3. Don't put faith in personal experience, tradition, or common sense. Only God's truth has the power to set you free. Read and memorize John 8:32.

4. You can defeat the devil with your words. Discover how Jesus did it by reading Matthew 4:1-11 and make a list of devil defeating words for your personal use.

5. Find out why it is smart to forgive those who have wronged you by reading the story of David's life before he was made king.

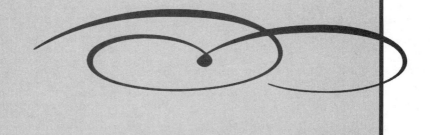

Chapter Four

DON'T LOSE HOPE!
YOU *CAN* HAVE
A NEW BEGINNING

DON'T LOSE HOPE! YOU *CAN* HAVE A NEW BEGINNING

As you look at the book of Ruth, you will discover how God provided a new beginning for Ruth and her mother-in-law, Naomi. You will learn how to make *exceptional* decisions that will bring forth the *extraordinary* from God in *your* life.

> *May the LORD repay you for what you have done. May you be richly rewarded by the LORD, the God of Israel, under whose wings you have come to take refuge*
> (Ruth 2:12 NIV).

Seemingly good reasons sometimes lead to bad choices and one bad decision can lead to another. Yet bad decisions, regardless of intentions, eventually have the same results—ruin in some areas of your life. When at last you discover yourself in desperate straits, and you want to "go home," it may look like "you can't get there from here."

If you feel that nothing good can come of your life…it's too late…things are hopeless—you're *wrong*. God wants to rescue you from your situation. He is the God of "new beginnings" and He *still* loves you. He can and He will put your life back on track…if you *allow* Him. God will build an expressway from where you are right now, directly to His plan for your life.

A Cursed Place

The events recorded in the book of Ruth took place during the time of Israel's judges (the period between the founding of the nation and its first king, approximately 500 years). The story begins in time of famine. There are 13 recorded famines in the Old Testament, including famines visited upon the children of Israel as judgment for turning away from God to worship idols. During this time of hardship, God dealt with the hearts of the men and women of the nation to return to Him.

Rather than remain and look to the Lord for their needs, Elimelech took his wife Naomi and their two sons, Mahlon and Chillion, to Moab. Elimelech made a bad decision, because God had cursed the nation of Moab. Perhaps his intentions were good, possibly to better provide for his small family, but regardless, this bad choice cost him his life and the lives of his two sons.

Modern-day Jordan would be a part of ancient Moab. The people of Moab were the descendants of the daughters of Lot, Abraham's nephew, who had incestuous relations with their father while fleeing God's destruction of the wicked city of Sodom. The people of Moab worshiped an idol called Chemosh, whom God calls "the abomination of Moab." *Chemosh* means a "dunghill deity." Whether Naomi's husband was running away from God or looking for a better job, this foul place with its blasphemous "god" is the land to which he brought his family. We, too, can step out of God's plan for our lives with a bad choice, even if it's made for the best of reasons.

"Return to Me"

*I will give them a heart to know me, that I am
the LORD. They will be my people, and I will
be their God, for they will return to me with
all their heart* (Jeremiah 24:7 NIV).

The book of Ruth chronicles a "new beginning" for
two women caught up in a tragedy. It shows how *the decisions
we make determine our
destiny*—how choices,
not chance, guide the
events of our lives. God
has a divine plan for
your life that is
wonderful and full of
His blessing, but the
devil also has a plan for
you—and his dirty
destiny for you is ruin.
Your choices determine
whose path you will

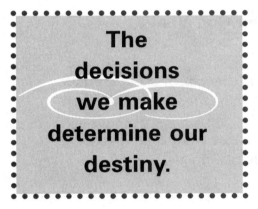

The
decisions
we make
determine our
destiny.

take and whose future you will live under.

Perhaps Naomi's husband thought they would spend
only a few months, or at most a year, in Moab; but one poor
choice led to another and ten years later the husband and
both sons were dead, and Naomi had nothing but regrets.
One bad choice, *seemingly* small and reversible, can often
lead to a lifestyle that excludes God, but includes tragedy.

As parents, the wrong choices we make can also set
the course for our children. While in Moab, both of Naomi's

sons took women of that country for wives. In their own culture, such a marriage could not have taken place without the consent of Naomi and her husband. By marrying women who were not Jews, Naomi's sons broke the law of God's covenant and stepped even farther from God's blessing. In that culture, as in many today, a young man brought his wife home to live with his family, so both of Naomi's daughters-in-law lived in her house. The day came when Naomi woke up, looked around, saw that she no longer had a reason to live in Moab, and realized her best option was to return to her home in Bethlehem.

When God Visits

> *Then she arose with her daughters-in-law that she might return from the country of Moab, for she had heard in the country of Moab that* **the LORD had visited His people** *by giving them bread* (Ruth 1:6 NKJ).

The expression, God "visited His people" is found throughout the Bible. When God visits, He always brings a blessing. In this instance, God ended the famine by providing a bountiful harvest.

In the New Testament, when speaking about the gentile revival that began with Simon Peter's visit to the house of Cornelius, James said:

> *Simeon hath declared how God at the first did* **visit the Gentiles,** *to take out of them a people for his name* (Acts 15:14).

God's greatest visit was that of His Son, who was born as a baby, grew up to be a man, and took upon Himself our sins and the sins of a lost world. Speaking of Jesus before His birth, Zacharias, the father of John the Baptist, said:

> *Blessed is the Lord God of Israel, for* **He has visited and redeemed His people,...**
> (Luke 1:68 NKJ).

If welcomed, God will visit those who are hopelessly mired in the quicksand of sin, and He promises to set them free. In Zephaniah 2:7 it says, *"...for the LORD their God* ***shall visit them, and turn away their captivity."***

Two Choices...Two Consequences

Every situation we face in life presents two possible choices—we can decide to do what is *expected* or what is *exceptional*. The *expected* choice is the easiest and most comfortable route to take, and provides an *expected* result. However, when we choose to do the *exceptional*, we open the way for God to do the *extraordinary* in our lives.

Naomi and her daughters-in-law were on the verge of determining their destinies. God wanted to bring great blessing into their lives. However, it was up to them to decide whether to do the *expected* or the *exceptional*, and their choices would determine their destinies. If you are like me, you do not want the *expected* outcome in your life; you crave the *extraordinary*! Watch Ruth! She makes an *exceptional* choice that makes possible a "new beginning" for herself and Naomi.

As Naomi was preparing to leave Moab to return home, she discouraged her daughters-in-law from coming with her because she had no future to offer them. In their culture, they would normally have married the brothers of their late husbands, but Naomi had no other sons. She told them, "Go home to your families and find another man to marry. It's the best thing for you."

One daughter-in-law, Orpah, made the *expected* decision, did the "common sense" thing, and returned to her parents' home. However, the other daughter-in-law, Ruth, obviously loved Naomi a great deal, wanted to share her life for better or worse, and refused to leave her. *Ruth,* whose name means "beautiful," uttered some of the most beautiful words found in Holy Scripture when she declared her devotion to Naomi:

> *...Entreat me not to leave you, or to turn back from following after you; for wherever you go, I will go; and wherever you lodge, I will lodge; your people shall be my people, and your God, my God. Where you die, I will die, and there will I be buried. The LORD do so to me, and more also, if anything but death parts you and me* (Ruth 1:16,17 NKJ).

When Ruth said, "your God" will be "my God," the word for God is *Elohim. Elohim* is the creator of the universe, a God of might and awesome power. However, when Ruth said, "The LORD," she used the word *Jehovah,* and *Jehovah* is your *personal* God. By her words, Ruth had turned away from the idol Chemosh and turned to the true and living God.

Ruth chose to do the *exceptional,* and wait until you see the *extraordinary* things God did in her life!

"El" Who?

Make no mistake, Ruth and Naomi were real people; they were not characters in a book. When they arrived in Bethlehem, they were hot, sweaty, covered with dust, and footsore. These were not the "little women" of the Bible; they were living, breathing people with the same faults, fears, and desires you and I have. Their arrival in Bethlehem caused a great commotion; many people turned out to greet them. When asked how she was doing, Naomi replied:

Naomi means pleasant, but Mara means bitter.

> *...Do not call me Naomi; call me Mara, for the Almighty has dealt very bitterly with me. I went out full, and the LORD has brought me home again empty. Why do you call me Naomi, since the LORD has testified against me, and the Almighty has afflicted me?* (Ruth 1:20,21 NKJ).

The name *Naomi* means "pleasant," but *Mara* means "bitter." By renaming herself, Naomi is declaring that when she left Bethlehem she had everything, she is now returning with nothing, and her loss has made her a *bitter* person. When *you* reach the end of the wrong path, you, too, may have lost not only your innocence but your sweetness and joy. However, like Naomi, the day will come when you can "reclaim your name."

By complaining and blaming God for her problems, Naomi did the *expected;* however, even in her despair and grief, Naomi planted a seed of hope by using the word "Almighty." *El Shaddai* is the name of God that is translated "Almighty." I'm sure you recall that El Shaddai is the aspect of God Who does the impossible, Who is more than enough to meet any need, the Bringer of the *extra*ordinary.

In the natural, there was no hope for Naomi to have a good life—she had no assets, nothing but another mouth to feed—her daughter-in-law. As was common to women of her culture, Naomi's greatest desire was to be a grandmother and have her lineage continue through a child. However, her sons were dead and she was too old to bear another. Things seemed hopeless. Instead of *truly* giving up, Naomi did a small but *exceptional* thing; she received revelation and called to God as "El Shaddai."

If your life seems hopeless and you feel helpless, *you* can begin now to do something small but *exceptional.* You can—stop blaming and start hoping in God, put your life into God's hands, receive salvation, renew your relationship with Him, begin to attend church, start reading the Word every day, and make time to spend alone in prayer with Him. Like Naomi, take that first small step toward your new beginning, do something small but *exceptional!*

Lay Anchor

*That by two immutable things, in which it was impossible for God to lie, we might have a strong consolation, who have fled for refuge to lay hold upon the hope set before us: Which hope we have as an **anchor of the soul**,...* (Hebrews 6:18-19).

Your hope needs an anchor. Naomi clung to a small hope that God would intervene in her situation: *El Shaddai* was her anchor. You need an anchor too. Perhaps sometime in the past, God brought you through a difficult situation, healed you, or gave you favor with others. Perhaps a scripture spoke in a special way to you, or in some way God showed His love for you. Any of those things might be considered your anchor.

He is a God of hope:

*May the **God of hope** fill you with all joy and peace as you trust in him, so that you may overflow with hope by the power of the Holy Spirit* (Romans 15:13 NIV).

It's *Your* Choice

Naomi was depressed. She was old, poor, and had no way to care for herself. Naomi was grieving; she had lost her husband and two sons. When people lose loved ones, it is expected that they will grieve. In every culture, death is an occasion for grief, usually expressed in some kind of sad funeral ritual. When a believer dies and goes to God, it is understandable that we, too, would feel sad because we will miss seeing them for a while, but we have the consolation of knowing that our separation is only *temporary,* not permanent.

Therefore, we should take the focus off *our* loss and rejoice for the "gain" of the one who has gone "home." After all, the battles and difficulties have ended; the goal has been achieved when someone we love has gone on to a great reward. We should celebrate this "move up"! Instead of embracing a depressing time of extended bereavement, we should relinquish our grief and sorrow, and give them to Jesus. Perhaps if we are *exceptional* in this, we will receive the *extraordinary*!

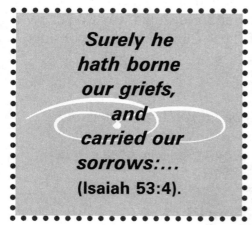

Surely he hath borne our griefs, and carried our sorrows:... (Isaiah 53:4).

You may be thinking, "grieving is important, it's a part of the process of dealing with death," and I agree. There is a time for grieving. I've lost loved ones myself, and have gone through a time of grieving, but I've also felt joy and victory when a loved one passed away, knowing that God's way was the best. The same Jesus who carried your sins also *bore your grief and carried your sorrow.* Unlike Naomi, you and I have a choice, we can let Jesus have our grief and carry our sorrow—or carry it ourselves.

Pillar of the Community

So Naomi returned, and Ruth the Moabitess her daughter-in-law with her, who returned from the country of Moab. Now they came to Bethlehem at the beginning of barley harvest (Ruth 1:22 NKJ).

Harvest time was a good time to return to Bethlehem because, except in years of famine, there was plenty of food to eat at that time of year. That year, God had given them an excellent harvest. By Hebrew law, landowners were required to allow the poor and needy to follow the reapers during harvest time, so they could gather the fallen and leftover grain.

One of the wealthiest landowners of the city, Boaz, came from the notable family of Elimelech. Boaz was a rich relative of Naomi's deceased husband. His name is interesting because it is the same as the name given to one of the two pillars standing in the temple that Solomon built. (Solomon's temple was actually more "David's temple" because it was David who purchased the site, and was the one whom God gave the plans and the gold with which to build it.)

The name *Boaz* means, "in Him is strength." The other pillar in the temple was called *Jachin* which means, "He will establish." Walking into the temple and seeing these pillars, a believer was tremendously reassured, knowing God would *strengthen* and *establish* His people. Solomon erected them in memory of the two pillars that led the Israelites to the Promised Land—the "pillar of fire" by night and the "pillar of cloud" by day. Boaz was a "pillar of the community," an *exceptional* kind of guy.

REDEEM

The Book of Ruth is a beautiful account of the kinsman-redeemer. His responsibility is summed up in Ruth 4:5: *"What day thou buyest the field of the hand of Naomi, thou must buy it also of Ruth the Moabitess, the wife of the dead, to raise up the name of the dead upon his inheritance."* Thus the kinsman-redeemer was responsible for preserving the integrity, life, property, and family name of his close relative or for executing justice upon his murderer.

(Reprinted by permission from *Vine's Expository Dictionary of Biblical Words* © 1985, Thomas Nelson Publishers)

Happenstance? Or Divine Rendezvous

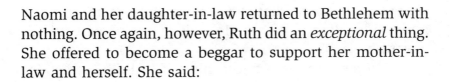

Naomi and her daughter-in-law returned to Bethlehem with nothing. Once again, however, Ruth did an *exceptional* thing. She offered to become a beggar to support her mother-in-law and herself. She said:

> ..."Please let me go to the field, and glean heads of grain after him in whose sight I may find favor." And she said to her, "Go, my daughter." Then she left, and went and gleaned in the field after the reapers. And **she happened to come to the part of the field belonging to Boaz,** who was of the family of Elimelech (Ruth 2:2,3 NKJ).

Ruth didn't just "happen" to come to Boaz's field. This was far more than "good luck"; divine destiny was at work. Had Ruth not done the *exceptional* and instead stayed at home being a "couch potato" catching up on the "soaps" that day, she would never have met and impressed Boaz. God wants to meet *your* needs, He wants to answer *your* prayers, however, you have to get out in the "fields" and give Him the *opportunity* to do the *extraordinary*.

Boaz had traveled there to see how the harvesting was going, and he almost immediately noticed beautiful Ruth working in his field. Boaz asked his foreman who this stranger was and discovered that she was Naomi's daughter-in-law. The *expected* thing would have been for Boaz to do nothing other than ask out of curiosity. Everyone knew Naomi's sad story and Boaz was filled with compassion for her circumstances. Then he saw Ruth and was impressed by her hard work and humble manner. Boaz commanded his foreman to look out for Ruth's safety among the rough farmhands, and to make sure that she reaped a good harvest. He even suggested that the reapers drop extra grain on purpose for Ruth to gather. He took an *exceptional* attitude toward her.

When Boaz introduced himself to Ruth, something very special happened. He said to Ruth:

> *...You will listen, my daughter, will you not? Do not go to glean in another field, nor go from here, but stay close by my young women. Let your eyes be on the field which they reap, and go after them. Have I not commanded the young men not to touch you? And when you are thirsty, go to the vessels and drink from what the young men have drawn* (Ruth 2:8,9 NKJ).

Since he calls her, "my daughter," it is likely that Boaz was old enough to relate to Ruth as if she were his daughter. He saw her vulnerability but, rather than take advantage of her, Boaz related to her in a way proper for a man his age, as father to daughter—seeing to her security and making her work as comfortable as possible.

Ruth was so overwhelmed by his gallantry that she...

> *...fell on her face, bowed down to the ground, and said to him, "Why have I found favor in your eyes, that you should take notice of me, since I am a foreigner?"* (Ruth 2:10 NKJ).

Ruth was not just flirting by asking the question

concerning "favor in your eyes." This was a genuine and legitimate question since Boaz's concern for her came as a complete surprise. Ruth was nothing to Boaz; she had no legal claim upon his good will. She was a stranger in a land where strangers, if allowed to remain, were often treated with open suspicion and hostility. In addition, her home country had been at war with the Israelites on and off for years, making her an enemy. What is more, Ruth knew that Boaz was a rich and powerful man and she needed to understand whether or not there were conditions for his "favor" and, if so, what form of repayment he might expect of her.

> *And Boaz answered and said to her, "It has been fully reported to me, all that you have done for your mother-in-law since the death of your husband, and how you have left your father and your mother and the land of your birth, and have come to a people whom you did not know before. The LORD repay your work, and a full reward be given you by the LORD God of Israel, under whose wings you have come for refuge"* (Ruth 2:11,12 NKJ).

The Exceptional Gets Noticed

When *we* do the exceptional, people notice. Boaz complimented Ruth on her almost sacrificial devotion to Naomi, and respected her decision to leave her homeland and parents to come to the land of her enemy. He went on to say that God looked favorably upon her sacrifice and would reward her for it by giving her refuge under His wings.

Boaz answered Ruth's question about the cost of his generosity by implying that he was merely an agent for God's favor. In other words, he had no *personal* motives in helping her and Naomi, and he expected nothing in return.

Ruth then thanked Boaz, saying something very sweet:

> *"May I continue to find favor in your eyes, my lord," she said. "You have given me comfort and have spoken kindly to your servant— though I do not have the standing of one of your servant girls"* (Ruth 2:13 NIV).

One translation says, *"...you have spoken to the heart of your maidservant."* His words were perhaps the kindest anyone had spoken to her since coming to Bethlehem, and their sincerity touched her heart. Ruth recognized Boaz as a truly exceptional man.

In God's Pocket

When lunchtime came, Boaz invited Ruth to eat with him and his farmhands at their table, and served her himself. Watch closely now. Ruth did a small thing that was very exceptional:

> *...So she sat beside the reapers, and he passed parched grain to her; and she ate and was satisfied, and kept some back* (Ruth 2:14 NKJ).

Ruth "kept some back," she put some of the food *in her pocket*. (Soon we will discover why she saved the food.)

In the meantime, they finished lunch and went back

to work. Boaz told his men, "Ruth doesn't have to take the leftover grain, allow her to reap wherever she likes. In fact, take some of what you have gathered and intentionally drop it for her to retrieve." At this point, her *exceptional* decisions are beginning

> **If you are like me, you do not want the *expected* outcome in your life; you crave the *extraordinary*!**

to bring the *extraordinary* into her life. It's the same for you. When you do the *exceptional,* you can *expect the extraordinary* in return.

By the time Ruth had finished her hard day in the fields, "beating out the grain," she had an *ephah* (almost two-thirds of a bushel) of barley. That was incredible! In one day, Ruth had earned the equivalent of a half-month's wage!

What did Ruth do with this new wealth? Did she take it to the market and trade it for a new red dress? No, she took it to her mother-in-law.

Remember the food from lunch that Ruth kept back? It was for Naomi!

> ... *She brought out and gave to her what she had kept back after she had been satisfied* (Ruth 2:18 NKJ).

Ruth said, "Naomi, I had the best lunch. I just had to pocket some of it and bring it to you." Ruth was tired and sore from a hard day's work, and could have said, "While you've been sitting around the house I've worked from sunrise to sunset. Where is my dinner?" Rather, she brought back everything—including what was in her pocket—and gave it to her mother-in-law.

Have you ever noticed the *small acts of kindness* God does for us? Like Ruth, He often saves "little lumps of goodness" in His pocket to share with *us*. These are not big, dramatic things that will change our lives, but small things that can inspire joy and change our day. We do the same kind of thing for *our* children. If we're shopping and see a small thing that we just know our child would love, we stop and get it for them. These small acts of kindness are evidence of God's fatherly love towards us. If we don't pay attention, we might think these "good things" are merely accidental good fortune.

Love Covenant

> ...*the LORD who has not withdrawn his kindness* [checed] *to the living and to the dead...* (Ruth 2:20 NAS).

The word often translated "kindness" from the original Hebrew is *checed,* and refers to God's covenant of love with His people. In this covenant, God has promised to love us unconditionally—forever. *Checed* is translated in the King James Version "mercy, kindness, or lovingkindness" and has within it the thought of a strong obligation (contract) to steadfastly love. Out of God's great love flows grace and mercy.

God's love for us is not a whimsy or temporary condition, and it goes far deeper than romantic love, which often depends upon physical appearance. Checed is based upon a mutually binding relationship between God and man, which surpasses the obligation to act with generosity and mercy. Checed is a personal relationship *and* covenant.

God's covenant of love with us is best expressed in Hebrews 13:5:

> *...He [God] Himself has said, I will not in any way fail you nor give you up nor leave you without support. [I will] not, [I will] not, [I will] not in any degree leave you helpless nor forsake nor let [you] down...* (TAB).

God had a contract of checed (love) with His chosen people. Ruth, as a member of the cursed nation of Moab, was outside that covenant. However, early in the story, when Naomi prepared to send her daughters-in-law away, she gave them a *covenant* blessing by saying:

> *...Go, return each to her mother's house: the LORD deal kindly* [checed] *with you, as ye have dealt with the dead, and with me* (Ruth 1:8).

By refusing to leave Naomi and declaring, "*...your people shall be my people, and your God, my God*" (Ruth 1:16 NKJ), Ruth turned away from the idol Chemosh to the Living God of Israel and called Him *her* Lord. At that moment, Ruth came under the contract of Love.

The very moment that *you* receive forgiveness for your sins and declare Jesus Lord of your life, you, too, come under God's covenant of love and qualify to receive His mercy and grace.

Reaping Your Harvest

When Ruth told her mother-in-law about the exceptional favor she had received from Boaz, a spark of hope ignited in Naomi's heart and renewed her faith in God's love covenant with her. Naomi was beginning to change.

> *...Then Ruth told her mother-in-law about the one at whose place she had been working. "The name of the man I worked with today is Boaz," she said. "The LORD bless him!" Naomi said to her daughter-in-law. "He has not stopped showing his kindness to the living and the dead." She added, "That man is our close relative; he is one of our kinsman-redeemers"* (Ruth 2:19,20 NIV).

Ruth was obedient both to Boaz and to Naomi. Throughout the barley and the wheat harvest, she stayed in Boaz's fields and continued to work with his female employees. Had Ruth thought and acted the *expected* way, she might have decided Boaz was too old a man to interest her, and might have gone to work in other fields where she could meet a variety of young eligible men. After all, she was young and beautiful, and it most certainly would have crossed her mind that it would be beneficial to remarry someone who would help provide for her.

Naomi's Good Advice

Naomi's attitude began to change dramatically once she saw the hand of God providing for her needs and those of Ruth. Her trust in God and His covenant began to grow, and soon she was inspired to give good, godly advice to Ruth. Naomi could have continued in her grief, blaming God for her problems but, having seen God's favor at work, Naomi was ready to give *exceptional* advice.

Knowing that harvest time had ended, Naomi wanted to see Ruth cared for and established in a secure marriage. She suggested that Ruth propose marriage to Boaz! Now, this was *very* unusual in their culture, as it is in most, and it was complicated by the fact that Boaz was a kinsman of Naomi's late husband. To marry Ruth, Boaz would have to agree to become a kinsman-redeemer.

While Ruth surely had a desire to find that "special someone" and settle down, get out of the fields, and have a home and children, this suggestion must have really shocked her. However, she had prayed and waited, and now recognized that Naomi gave her godly advice. I've said it before, but it bears repeating—*wait* on God for the answers to *your* prayers.

Naomi told Ruth what to do:

> *Is not Boaz, with whose servant girls you have been, a kinsman of ours? Tonight he will be winnowing barley on the threshing floor. Wash and perfume yourself, and put on your best clothes. Then go down to the*

> *threshing floor, but don't let him know you are there until he has finished eating and drinking. When he lies down, note the place where he is lying. Then go and uncover his feet and lie down. He will tell you what to do." "I will do whatever you say," Ruth answered* (Ruth 3:2-5 NIV).

Can you imagine Ruth's excitement, a mixture of fear of rejection and the anticipation of a bride, as she bathed and carefully prepared herself to go to the threshing floor? She must have had a knot of tension in the pit of her stomach as she hid in the shadows of the flickering lamps that lit the threshing floor, watching every move that Boaz made. Then, once the lights were extinguished, the minutes until Boaz went to sleep must have seemed like hours as she looked toward the dark shadow where he lay. Then, carefully, she had to thread her way among the other sleepers to the feet of Boaz. Not knowing whether she would be accepted or rejected, she must have laid herself down at his feet in great fear, perhaps even trembling.

God's Meeting Place—the Threshing Floor

Threshing floors have special significance to God. Perhaps you remember the story of Gideon and how God sent an angel to meet him at the threshing floor. The angel said to Gideon, *"...The LORD is with you, you mighty man of valor!"* (Judges 6:12 NKJ). Gideon as much as cried, "Who *me*? I'm not valorous!" Nevertheless, from that *threshing floor*, God was able to take a reluctant Gideon and turn

The Threshing Floor

In addition to being a place where grain was processed to separate seed from hull, the threshing floor was a place of thanksgiving to God, where Hebrews showed gratitude to God for His *grace* through "heave offerings":

You shall offer up a cake of the first of your ground meal as a heave offering; as a heave offering of the threshing floor, so shall you offer it up (Numbers 15:20 NKJ).

This form of "peace offering" was to remind the Hebrews, while they were enjoying His bounty, that the "good things" in their lives were due to God's amazing grace.

him into a "mighty man" who, with only 300 men, defeated an army of 135,000.

If you feel powerless standing against the overwhelming odds of your situation as Gideon did, you can take hope from Gideon's God. He *loves* it when the odds against us are overwhelming because it gives Him an opportunity to demonstrate His supernatural power in a mighty way to give us the victory. Paul understood the secret of dealing with "the overwhelming," he said, *"...when I am weak, then am I strong"* (II Corinthians 12:10).

The threshing floor was prominent in David's story, too. David's affair with Bathsheba wasn't his only mistake. On one occasion, against God's explicit instructions, David decided to take a census and number the people of Israel. He wanted to know how many fighting men he could count on for his next war. David's disobedience loosed the sword of the angel of death over Israel, and tens of thousands died until David repented of his disobedience and offered a sacrifice to God upon the *threshing floor* of Ornan the Jebusite. David purchased that same threshing floor and, years later, upon that altar, Solomon erected his beautiful temple to God.

Have you made some mistakes? Have you knowingly done things contrary to God's will? If your disobedience has loosed a whirlwind of destruction into *your* life, you can stop the destruction now and make a *threshing floor* wherever you are by getting on your knees to repent. Out of your repentance, God will build a temple, something of great beauty and value in your life.

The threshing floor of Bethlehem became a meeting place for Ruth and Boaz, and something extraordinary happened there at midnight.

In The Dead of Night

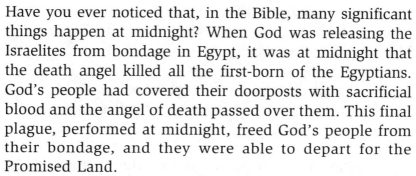

Have you ever noticed that, in the Bible, many significant things happen at midnight? When God was releasing the Israelites from bondage in Egypt, it was at midnight that the death angel killed all the first-born of the Egyptians. God's people had covered their doorposts with sacrificial blood and the angel of death passed over them. This final plague, performed at midnight, freed God's people from their bondage, and they were able to depart for the Promised Land.

At midnight, Samson—the Bible's strongest man— caused incredible destruction to the enemies of Israel. In the New Testament, God chose the hour of midnight to work a very great miracle. After being severely beaten and put in stocks, Paul and Silas found they couldn't sleep so they put the time to good use:

> *About midnight Paul and Silas were praying and singing hymns to God, and the other prisoners were listening to them. Suddenly there was such a violent earthquake that the foundations of the prison were shaken. At once all the prison doors flew open, and everybody's chains came loose* (Acts 16:25,26 NIV).

If you are at a "midnight point" in your life, worrying and pacing the floor, know that you can have victory in your darkest hour! Do what Paul and Silas did. Begin to pray and praise God and watch the foundations shake and *your* chains fall off!

God has chosen midnight to describe the time for the greatest event in mankind's history—the hour when Jesus returns to earth to receive His bride, the Church. When explaining His return to His disciples, Jesus encouraged them to be watching and ready. Using a parable, detailed in Matthew 25:6, Jesus said:

> *And at midnight a cry was heard: 'Behold, the bridegroom is coming; go out to meet him!' (NKJ).*

Whenever it happens, during the daytime or the evening, on that day, *all* of our troubles, trials, and tribulations will be ended as we meet Jesus.

The Wings of God

In the middle of the night something startled the man, and he turned and discovered a woman lying at his feet. "Who are you?" he asked. "I am your servant Ruth," she said. "Spread the corner of your garment over me, since you are a kinsman-redeemer." "The LORD bless you, my daughter," he replied. "This kindness is greater than that which you showed earlier: You have not run after the younger men, whether rich or poor. And now, my daughter, don't be afraid. I will do for you all you ask. All my fellow townsmen know that you are a woman of noble character (Ruth 3:8-11 NIV).

The last time Boaz talked to Ruth, He said:

*...May you be richly rewarded by the LORD,
the God of Israel, **under whose wings you have
come to take refuge*** (Ruth 2:12 NIV).

Boaz recognized that Ruth had entered into a covenant
relationship with God and was entitled to take refuge under
His "wings." The wings of God were represented by the
golden wings of the cherumbin that covered the mercy seat,
located in the Holy of Holies of God's temple. Mercy is a
part of our Love Covenant. Under God's wings is a place of
security and safety.

Ruth replied by asking Boaz also to be her "covering."
She said, "I want to be your wife, to be under *your* wing." It
is customary at a Jewish wedding for the man to put his
robe around his bride, saying that he will be her covering.

Boaz did not reject her. No! He felt delighted and
privileged to be offered the opportunity to be the husband
and kinsman-redeemer of this virtuous, beautiful young
woman. However, Boaz was also required to provide Naomi
a place in his household, knowing that any child that came
from his union with Ruth would carry the name of Mahlon,
Ruth's dead husband. Boaz clearly did something exceptional
by agreeing to marry Ruth.

Let's look at another exceptional thing that occurred
that night—or rather didn't occur—sex. Picture the scenario.
Boaz and Ruth were lying in the dark together. She was
young and beautiful, smelled of seductive perfumes, and
he had had a little to drink during the festivities. Naomi
had told Ruth to do whatever Boaz commanded—after all,
they would probably be married soon. All the ingredients

were there for a night of pleasure, but neither one gave into to their desires. Their *exceptional* restraint ensured an *extraordinary* marriage, and the same principle will work for you.

Now, before the wedding could occur, Boaz had a *problem* to resolve. There was another man more suited by tradition to serve as Ruth's kinsman-redeemer.

> *Although it is true that I am near of kin, there is a kinsman-redeemer nearer than I. Stay here for the night, and in the morning if he wants to redeem, good; let him redeem. But if he is not willing, as surely as the LORD lives I will do it. Lie here until morning." So she lay at his feet until morning, but got up before anyone could be recognized; and he said, "Don't let it be known that a woman came to the threshing floor"* (Ruth 3:12-14 NIV).

Before first light, Ruth arose to leave. Boaz also got up and, in a hushed voice, told her not to mention to anyone that she had spent the night at the threshing floor. Then, as a gift, he gave her all the barley she could carry and sent her home to Naomi.

Which of the people in this story do you suppose slept the most that night? Possibly, Boaz got the most sleep—and that was only the short rest before Ruth awoke him by uncovering his feet! It is doubtful that Ruth slept at all. She must have tossed and turned, considering what the next day would bring, and wondering what the man (whose feet were now next to her) would be like as a husband. Boaz must have been deluged with love and desire for his young *potential* bride, planning how he would deal with the man who was closest kin. I suspect Boaz, being a godly man, prayed for God to give him wisdom the next day. At any rate, he was awake when Ruth got up to leave.

Naomi, too, probably stayed awake all night, worrying how things were going at the threshing floor. Perhaps she allowed her hope to increase as the hours passed, but by the time Ruth quietly entered the house, Naomi was wide-awake and asked:

> *...How did it go, my daughter? Then she told her everything Boaz had done for her and added, He gave me these six measures of barley, saying, "Don't go back to your mother-in-law empty-handed." Then Naomi said, "Wait, my daughter, until you find out what happens. For the man will not rest until the matter is settled today"* (Ruth 3:16-18 NIV).

The Redeemer Who Wasn't

Let me remind you again that choices determine destiny. The *exceptional* choices Ruth made brought her to the brink of realizing all her dreams. Had she stayed in Moab and returned to her parents, it would have been much *easier* to find a new husband. Never during the process did it seem that her dreams would be fulfilled. Rather than strive for what she *wanted*, however, she did what was *right*.

Under the Law

According to Hebrew law, a man could not sell his farm property as we do—free and clear with no future claim upon it. Rather, a man was allowed only to sell the use of his land for a period of time, subject to redemption (or buy back).

Upon his death, his closest kin, or the current tenant of his property, could then purchase or redeem the property. In Naomi's case, her husband must have sold his property rights to another ten years earlier when she, her husband, and family left Bethlehem. Their sons or grandchildren would have been the only ones who could inherit the property of her dead husband. Her sons had died childless though, and now Ruth was the only person who could provide heirs for the continuation of the ownership of the property.

To gain the property, the kinsman-redeemer was required not only to pay a sum of money to the one who owned the property-use rights, but also had to marry Ruth and give her a son to ensure the continuation of the line of ownership and descent. Obviously, not every kinsman would have the desire to enter this legal and personal relationship.

Ruth's love for Naomi motivated her to remain with her mother-in-law and leave the familiar for an unknown and possibly hostile land. This first *exceptional* choice must have seemed to Ruth to actually be a step away from her desires. When *you* do the "right thing," it often feels like a step in the *wrong* direction, doesn't it? Unlike Ruth though, you have the assurance of the Lord that if you *"...acknowledge Him,* [in everything you do]*...He shall direct your paths* (Proverbs 3:6 NKJ).

Lest you think that Boaz was just "doing his duty" as a possible kinsman-redeemer, consider the clever (but honest way) he dealt with the "close relative" who had the *first* right to be Ruth's husband.

> *Meanwhile Boaz went up to the town gate and sat there. When the kinsman-redeemer he had mentioned came along, Boaz said, "Come over here, my friend, and sit down." So he went over and sat down. Boaz took ten of the elders of the town and said, "Sit here," and they did so. Then he said to the kinsman-redeemer, "Naomi, who has come back from Moab, is selling the piece of land that belonged to our brother Elimelech. I thought I should bring the matter to your attention and suggest that you buy it in the presence of these seated here and in the presence of the elders of my people. If you will redeem it, do so. But if you will not, tell me, so I will know. For no one has the right to do it except you, and I am next in line." "I will redeem it," he said* (Ruth 4:1-4 NIV).

As you probably know, the city gate was historically the place where official business was transacted. In this verse, we see God outlining a *new beginning* for Naomi, Ruth, and even Boaz. The man Boaz was waiting for also happened to be related to Naomi's husband—perhaps a cousin or uncle. Boaz might have waited all day, but the kinsman arrived immediately. Boaz invited him to sit down and asked several elders to join them as witnesses.

Initially, all Boaz talked about was the land; he didn't mention the young and beautiful Ruth. He told his kinsman that Naomi was ready to sell her land.

In Biblical times, land was more valuable than currency. Because each son inherited an equal portion of his father's land and, in turn, each of his sons inherited an equal portion and so on and on, after several hundred years of this practice with no new land available, land was at a premium. Boaz knew that his kinsman would jump at the opportunity to increase his holdings. As soon as his kinsman said, "Yes, I'll buy the land," Boaz said:

> ...*On the day you buy the land from Naomi and from Ruth the Moabitess, you acquire the dead man's widow, in order to maintain the name of the dead with his property* (Ruth 4:5 NIV).

Boaz reminded his kinsman that the price for this property included an obligation to provide for Naomi, take a new wife, and produce a son to carry on the name of Ruth's dead husband. He pointed out that after purchasing the property, assuming all the obligations, the property would still belong to Ruth's future son. After short consideration the kinsman said, "No:"

> *...Then I cannot redeem it because I might endanger my own estate. You redeem it yourself. I cannot do it* (Ruth 4:6 NIV).

The clever Boaz, with God's help, was now positioned to be Ruth's kinsman-redeemer.

The kinsman who allowed Boaz to claim the land made a wise decision based upon what was *best* for him. It's not likely that God did anything *extraordinary* for that kinsman based upon his *expected* decision. *Expected* decisions are always based upon what is *best* for us; *exceptional* decisions are based upon what is *best* for God or, through Him, for other people.

It's a Deal

> *(Now in earlier times in Israel, for the redemption and transfer of property to become final, one party took off his sandal and gave it to the other. This was the method of legalizing transactions in Israel.) So the kinsman-redeemer said to Boaz, "Buy it yourself." And he removed his sandal* (Ruth 4:7,8 NIV).

I've always been intrigued by this description of sealing a deal by giving a shoe to a person who purchased or redeemed a property. Wondering how the custom began, I looked in several scholarly resources but didn't find a satisfying answer. After praying, I believe God has given me insight into this custom. The foot in the Bible is a very strong symbol of ownership, domination, and power. Perhaps you remember God's promise to the Israelites before entering the Promised Land, *"Every place that the sole of your foot will tread upon I have given you,..."* (Joshua 1:3 NKJ). God was saying, what your shoe steps on is yours.

> *"Every place that the sole of your foot will tread upon I have given you,..."* (Joshua 1:3 NKJ).

Jesus has a promise for *our* feet, too. He said:

> *Behold, I give unto you power to tread on serpents and scorpions, and over all the power of the enemy: and nothing shall by any means hurt you* (Luke 10:19 KJV).

As a born-again child of God, the devil no longer has power or authority over you. This verse declares that you are *not* the possession of the devil; rather, *you* have power and authority over *him*.

Do you remember how David fled Jerusalem when his son, Absalom, was trying to take his throne? The Bible says that David left weeping and *barefoot*. David had taken his shoes off to show that he no longer ruled the land.

When God commanded Isaiah to weep over Israel—

Judah, in particular—because of all the evil doings there, Isaiah went barefoot. By removing his sandals, he indicated that Israel's favor with God had been removed because of the people's idolatry.

When the kinsman gave his shoe to Boaz, he was saying, "I give up all claim of possession to Naomi's land and upon Ruth and give it to you."

God Does the Extraordinary

Then Boaz announced to the elders and all the people, "Today you are witnesses that I have bought from Naomi all the property of Elimelech, Kilion and Mahlon. I have also acquired Ruth the Moabitess, Mahlon's widow, as my wife, in order to maintain the name of the dead with his property, so that his name will not disappear from among his family or from the town records. Today you are witnesses!" (Ruth 4:9,10 NIV).

The same reasons that made redeeming Ruth a "bad deal" for the kinsman also made it a bad deal for Boaz. Why would this man do such an *exceptional* thing? He did it for Ruth and Naomi. Make no mistake, Boaz would get a young, beautiful and virtuous wife but, as an older man, he was not carried away by youthful passions. Boaz was a godly man who wanted to redeem the name and property of another man—possibly one he had never even known—because it was the *right thing to do*.

Boaz's decision was not to do the most profitable thing, but to do the *right* thing—and that *exceptional* decision enabled

God to do a very *EXTRAORDINARY* thing for Boaz. Watch now as God brings the supernatural to bear on the life of Boaz. When *you* make *exceptional* decisions, you, too, bring God's supernatural power to bear on the situations of your life.

Two prophecies were made for Boaz and Ruth:

> *Then the elders and all those at the gate said, "We are witnesses. May the LORD make the woman who is coming into your home like Rachel and Leah, who together built up the house of Israel. May you have standing in Ephrathah and be famous in Bethlehem* (Ruth 4:11 NIV).

God moved upon ordinary people to prophesy that Boaz, about to sire and raise a child who would not carry his name, would have a house like Abraham's, the patriarch of the nation of Israel—a fruitful, famous, and long-lived line of descendants. In addition, they foresaw that Boaz would become renowned in all of Israel, and famous in Bethlehem. Even if God had stopped there, Boaz would have been blessed beyond all that he could have ever hoped or dreamed, but God had even more to offer:

> *Through the offspring the LORD gives you by this young woman, may your family be like that of Perez, whom Tamar bore to Judah* (Ruth 4:12 NIV).

Who was Perez? Perez was one of the twin sons born of Tamar. Do you remember Tamar? She was a woman who was denied her legal rights to have a child by a brother of her dead husband. Tamar masqueraded as a prostitute and tricked her father-in-law, Judah, into making her pregnant. This story is difficult for people of our culture to understand, especially because Tamar was pronounced "righteous." From that union came the twins, Zarah and Perez. *Perez* became a very great man; many of the people who lived in Bethlehem were his descendants, and his name means "breakthrough." This prophecy meant that Boaz would have a "breakthrough family."

Dream Maker

God wants to make *your* dreams come true, too! Boaz's dreams were fulfilled; he married the beautiful and virtuous Ruth and fathered a child who would place them both in the genealogy of Jesus Christ. Although it's possible Boaz was too old to have children, God likes to use the weak things to show Himself strong. Whatever natural hindrances might have been in the way of Ruth conceiving, God removed them. The Bible says *"...and the LORD enabled her to conceive, and she gave birth to a son"* (Ruth 4:13 NIV).

Although Boaz gave up his right to have the child who would be considered a part of his own lineage, God did not. Nowhere in any of the genealogies of Christ is Ruth's first husband, Mahlon, mentioned. Throughout this story both Ruth and Boaz had made *exceptional* choices, and God rewarded them with a supernaturally conceived child.

Ruth married the most *exceptional* and certainly one of the wealthiest men in Bethlehem. As a convert

SACRIFICE

Both the Old Testament and the New Testament confirm that sacrifices were presented as a symbolic gesture. Man was obligated, because of his sin, to present offerings by which he gave another life in place of his own. These substitutes pointed forward to the ultimate substitute, Jesus Christ (Hebrews 10:1-18).

According to God's command, the animal sacrificed had to be physically perfect in age and condition. Through the perfection of this animal, perfection was presented to God. Ultimately, this symbolized the necessity for man to present himself perfect before God by presenting the perfect one in his place (1 Peter 1:18-19). The true Lamb of God, innocent of all sin, took away sin (John 1:29).

After the animal was selected and presented at the altar, the first act was the laying on of hands by the person presenting the offering. By this act the worshiper symbolically transferred his sin and

and exceptional person herself, she enjoyed the blessing of the Lord for the remainder of her life. In addition, she saw her desires for Naomi to be well taken care of and given an heir met. However, we know of at least one more *exceptional* thing Ruth did, and it earned her place in history as one of the five exceptional women mentioned in the genealogy of Christ. She gave up that which was perhaps dearest to her, and allowed her child to be raised by Naomi.

guilt to the sacrificial animal which stood in his place. The sacrifice symbolically pointed to the Savior who would do for the believer what he could not do for himself. He would take upon Himself sin and guilt and accomplish redemption for His people (Isaiah 53:4-12; Matthew 1:21).

In the great atonement festival, two goats depicted this redemptive act. One goat died, its death symbolizing how the ultimate sacrifice in the future would pay the penalty for the believer's sin. Its blood was applied to the MERCY SEAT in the HOLY OF HOLIES, symbolizing how the great sacrifice would cover man's sin, bring unworthy man into God's presence, and make full restitution to God. On the head of the second goat the priest symbolically conferred the sin of God's people. Then this goat, known as the SCAPEGOAT, was sent into the wilderness to symbolize the removal of the people's sin.

(Reprinted by permission from *Nelson's Illustrated Bible Dictionary* © 1986, Thomas Nelson Publishers)

Living to Die or Dying to Live?

And the women said unto Naomi, Blessed be the LORD, which hath not left thee this day without a kinsman, that his name may be famous in Israel. And he shall be unto thee a

> *restorer of thy life, and a nourisher of thine*
> *old age: for thy daughter in law, which loveth*
> *thee, which is better to thee than seven sons,*
> *hath born him* (Ruth 4:14,15).

When Naomi returned from Moab, she believed that she had returned home to die—she had left Israel "full" and returned "empty." With the death of her husband followed by the untimely dying of her sons before they could father children, Naomi was doomed to a life of disappointment and despair, but for God's intervention. You, also, may experience times when you feel that you are at the long end of a trail of disasters and can see no hope. You may even reach a point where you think life is over and that you are merely "living to die." However, God wants to bless you and give *you* a reason to live.

Look what God did for Naomi. The woman who could have no heir was given a child to rear and nourish with God's Word. He marked this child to restore her in her old age. God did the impossible for Naomi—He gave her a "new beginning." God rescued Naomi and He will rescue you when you begin to make *exceptional* choices as she did.

Your Kinsman-Redeemer

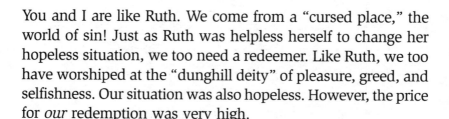

You and I are like Ruth. We come from a "cursed place," the world of sin! Just as Ruth was helpless herself to change her hopeless situation, we too need a redeemer. Like Ruth, we too have worshiped at the "dunghill deity" of pleasure, greed, and selfishness. Our situation was also hopeless. However, the price for *our* redemption was very high.

We needed to be bought back from sin. The price for sin has always been the blood of an innocent and pure sacrifice. To become our "kinsman-redeemer," Jesus had to leave His place beside the Father, divest Himself of His glory, and be born a man. He was, *"...tempted in every way, just as we are—yet was without sin"* (Hebrews 4:15 NIV). He took upon himself the sins of every person who had lived and those who were yet to come, and allowed His life to be painfully taken by the shedding of His blood. Jesus made this *exceptional* sacrifice to redeem us.

Why Would God Die for You?

What could be so important about *you* that God would send the One Who is dearest to Him to painfully give up His life for you? God personally knows you, and loves you so much that He wants to redeem (save) you from a life of slavery to sin. God paid the ultimate price in order to give you a new beginning.

Now what will *you* do? The *expected* thing would be to ignore the incredibly precious gift of redemption and continue as you are. However, it is within your power to reverse the curse of past mistakes. You *can* start today to take the first steps down the path to your "new beginning" by making an *exceptional* choice—choose life—turn to God.

The 5 Best Ways To...
Not Lose Hope!
You Can Have a New Beginning

1. List any hopeless situations you are currently facing. Next to each, list both "expected" and "exceptional" actions you might take to solve them. Pray for guidance on what to do.

2. Read in II Samuel 24 the story of David's sin and repentance at the threshing floor. Then read II Chronicles 3:1 and discover how God built something beautiful out of David's threshing floor experience.

3. Learn about doing the "right thing"—in this case publicly praying (even when it is difficult and seems counter-productive)—

by reading Daniel's story in Daniel chapter 6.

4. When God visits, He always brings a blessing! Write a letter to someone and describe something wonderful that God has done for you.

5. Put Matthew 6:33 to work on your "new beginning." Examine what you are putting "first" in your life and look for ways to "seek *first* His kingdom"—step up your prayer life, increase your Bible reading, attend church more often—do whatever you can to go *hard* after God.

Chapter Five

PLUG-IN TO THE "POWER SUPPLY"

PLUG-IN TO THE "POWER SUPPLY"

Have you ever been in a station that generates electrical power, where giant turbines produce tremendous quantities of energy? As these great machines turn, electrical current rushes through copper wires larger than a man's arm, producing a loud, pervasive "hum" that vibrates the floor and seems to throb to the depth of your bones.

For his Holy Spirit speaks to us deep in our hearts, and tells us that we really are God's children. And since we are his children, we will share his treasures—for all God gives to his Son Jesus is now ours too....

(Romans 8:16-17 TLB).

However, until massive switches direct the energy to where it will be used, all that power is useless. It just stays there, stored up, and accomplishes nothing.

God's power is greater than anything man can produce. It birthed the solar system, stars, and our own earth. The Bible says that God's power sustains our world to this day. However, like the electricity in a power station before it's redirected, God's power is only *potentially* useful in the situations of your life. It remains stored up until a switch is thrown open to redirect it into *actual* areas of need.

It was the Cross which put the giant turbines of God's grace into motion—and it is up to you to "plug into" this amazing power source and use it to light up your life!

Pakistani Power Surge

God has given me a heart for the Pakistani people. Recently, I had a large crusade planned for the city of Karachi, Pakistan. Pakistan is 98 percent Muslim, and Karachi, as you may know, is a hotbed of religious and civil unrest. Overcrowding, poverty, prejudice, sexism, anti-Americanism, and the routine persecution of Christians are accepted facts of life in this angry and seemingly hopeless nation. Time and again, the media carry reports of horrific burning, looting, and killing as the country's barely-suppressed rage boils over, cutting a swath of death and destruction through impoverished and helpless neighborhoods.

Flying home to Denver from a meeting, I was anticipating the coming crusade and remembering the other times I had ministered there.

During my first trip to Pakistan, I went to Lahore, though many of my ministry friends tried to discourage me, warning I might be kidnapped or killed. "A woman can't minister in a Muslim country," they declared. "Muslims won't come to your meetings!" In spite of their well-meaning but negative input, I felt that God wanted me go. During that first ministry event in Lahore, God *really* poured out blessings! No one in Pakistan knew my name before I arrived, but God brought a thousand people to my daytime seminars, and more than 40,000 attended the final night of that citywide, five-day crusade. It was an overwhelming victory for God in a Muslim country!

During the first trip, God completely exceeded my wildest hopes and highest dreams. Two years later, I returned and ministered in Pakistan's capital city, Islamabad. This time 2,600 pastors and Christian workers from all over the country joined us to attend our week-long Ministry Training School. The thing that really astonished me was the crowd of Muslims who attended the evening evangelistic, healing meetings. We started with 20,000 our first night, and by the closing night the crowd was conservatively estimated at 70,000 people! God ministered healing to thousands with unusual miracles! Tens of thousands of Muslims stood to receive Jesus in their hearts! The power that God manifested in those meetings was indescribable. It was the most awesome experience of my life! Just remembering it caused

Plug-in to God's amazing power source.

me to burn with excitement. I was *really* looking forward to what God would do on *this,* my third ministry trip to Pakistan.

My airplane landed safely in Denver, and while I was on my way home, the car phone rang. I was informed that we had just received a fax from our Pakistani event coordinator saying that the government permit to hold the crusade in Karachi had been canceled. Apparently, the government there was worried that they could not provide sufficient security and protection to ensure the safety of a Christian meeting—one where women would be ministering, no less! (It was scheduled to begin in ten days!)

We had been warned that the enemy had taken a special interest in this event and would make every effort to stop it. Now, it appeared Satan had succeeded. My event coordinator was scheduled to leave the following day for Pakistan, and I was asked to decide immediately whether he should proceed or wait. There was no time to formally "pray through" or "seek the Lord" for His will; there was only time to respond with either, "Yes, proceed and we will believe for a miracle," or "No, wait and see what happens."

As I mused over the bad news, I must say that canceling the crusade was never an option for me. Rather, my spirit was provoked with a fierce determination to see the devil's plans defeated and God's purpose for this event to succeed. I said, "Let's believe that God will make a way."

I asked our church, my ministry staff and partners, and everyone I knew to intercede for this crusade. My daughter and co-laborer in this ministry, Sarah Bowling, and I were supposed to leave for Pakistan in a few days, and so far the news had been all bad. Many people were working overtime to make things happen in Pakistan, but none of these efforts was bearing fruit.

When we arrived in Karachi, I learned that our request for permission had been put before the secretary to the Prime Minister, the second most powerful man in all of Pakistan. Everyone was hopeful, but still we did not have the necessary approval. We continued to pray and intercede.

The evening before the Ministry Training School was scheduled to begin, the meeting tent and other necessary things were in place, yet we still did not have approval for the crusade. That evening, I decided to go ahead with it, believing that we would receive the required approval in time.

The first day, we had wonderful teaching sessions in

the morning—but still the approval did not come. The afternoon sessions were powerful, and by the time they were concluded—we *had* it! Yes! We had the approval. God had moved the hearts of the nation's leaders, and they had given approval to hold our crusade! The enemy had brought to bear all his considerable influence and power in this Muslim country to disallow this meeting, but the power of prayer had broken his hold.

Satan had good reason to fear this event; it was a spiritual breakthrough for the city of Karachi. More than 2,500 pastors and Christian workers attended the daytime seminar, and each evening the crowds for the citywide crusades doubled and redoubled until the final night's attendance was well over 100,000 people—the largest Christian event *ever* held in Pakistan! I watched God lavish His healing power on the multitude, and saw thousands upon thousands of Muslims receive Jesus. People arrived in wheelchairs, upon beds, and were carried by ambulances from hospitals and walked out healed! It reminded me of the first days of the early church, when sick people were brought into the street so that Peter's shadow would fall upon and heal them!

After five incredible days, not a person in that city could deny that Jesus loved and healed Muslims. The name of Jesus flew high and proud like a banner over the city of Karachi during that time, and Satan's standard was trampled in the dirt by the countless feet that beat a path to the meeting grounds. There are no words to describe what God did there: miraculous, supernatural, phenomenal, awesome, and marvelous—all are inadequate! I'm humbled by the privilege that God gave me to be a part of His magnificent demonstration of love for the people of Karachi.

During the days of uncertainty before we had approval to hold the event, I was sure that we would win and that God would prevail. My belief wasn't based upon a Pollyanna-like denial of the facts, an exalted self-opinion, or a special "inside track" with God. Rather, my certainty was in the spiritual authority that was brought to bear against the enemy by God's people. Because of the *"cross*over," *every* Christian has spiritual authority over adverse situations and demonic circumstances.

What is a *"cross*over"? If you belong to Jesus, a *"cross*over" has occurred in your life that gives *you* the *authority* of a king, the *power* of a priest, and a double-portion *blessing*—the assurance that every promise in the Bible belongs to you. However, you must learn how to access the blessing and power which God's grace provides you through the "Great *Cross*over."

In the following pages, I'll share how God used the concept of *"cross*over" to change lives and accomplish His will on the earth.

Tra'dition, Tradition

Since earliest times it has been *traditional* in eastern countries for the first-born son to inherit the greater blessing of the priesthood, kingship, and birthright—the authority, power, and double portion inheritance. However, God occasionally intruded on man's traditions and conferred the first-born blessing upon a younger son. As far back as the time of Adam and Eve, Cain killed his brother Abel, lost his blessing, and so the blessing of the first-born came upon the third-born son, Seth.

In later times, had God followed traditions, He would have chosen Heron, the eldest son of Terah, over Abraham. Perhaps you think that God chose Abraham over his brothers because he was a great "man of God." Nothing could be farther from the truth. Abraham, like the people who lived around him, was an idolater who worshipped the moon. He didn't even live in the area that would later become Israel, but down in the land of Ur. However, God saw in Abraham a man who would *believe* Him: *"...Abraham believed God, and it was credited to him as righteousness"* (Romans 4:3 NIV). Abraham's faith in God grew so great that he was willing to offer his only son as a sacrifice—a forerunner to the *cross*over sacrifice of Jesus:

> A *"cross*over" gives *you* the *authority* of a king, the *power* of a priest, and a double-portion *blessing*.

> *By faith Abraham, when God tested him, offered Isaac as a sacrifice. He who had received the promises was about to sacrifice his one and only son,...* (Hebrews 11:17 NIV).

God has no "traditions" about whom should get His blessings; He doesn't play by our rules. God looks upon the *heart*. We sometimes think that education, IQ, physical appearance, or personality can make God favor one person over another. Wrong! God looks at *hearts*. God often uses and blesses the most unlikely people—and that gives hope to you and me. If you have a heart for God, you, too, are a candidate for a "*cross*over" blessing.

The Hacker and the Hunk

Abraham's *second* son, Isaac, was the son God had "promised," and the blessing crossed over the older and passed to the younger. Perhaps you recall the story: God promised Abraham and Sarah a son. However, when the promise wasn't fulfilled quickly enough, Abraham and Sarah decided to "help" God. Sarah suggested that Abraham father a child with her Egyptian maid, Hagar—a common practice in that culture. The result was Ishmael. He was Abraham's son of the *flesh*, but Isaac was the son of the *Spirit*. Once again, the younger ruled over the elder.

One of the most famous *cross*over blessings was that of Jacob and Esau. In this instance God prophesied to their mother, Rebecca, "*...and the elder shall serve the younger*" (Genesis 25:23). Esau and Jacob were fraternal twins. Esau was born first, and by tradition had the rights of the first-born to the kingly, priestly, and double-portion blessings.

If you had a chance to meet and compare these two brothers, you probably would have chosen Esau to receive God's blessing, just as he was Isaac's first choice. Esau was a macho kind of guy with a hairy chest. Today, he would probably be described as a "hunk" or a "jock." He liked manly pursuits and was a skilled hunter. Jacob, on the other hand, was a "thinker," and a crafty, devious one at that. In today's world, he might have been a computer hacker. He was hairless, and a real "mama's boy," too.

Somewhere along the line, probably while he was hanging onto Rebecca's apron strings, Jacob learned to cook—and he must have been pretty good at it. One day, Esau came home empty-handed and hungry from hunting, and the aroma of Jacob's home cooking threw him into a tailspin. He sold his birthright to Jacob for a bowl of beans! He was so sensual in nature that as soon as his stomach growled, he lost all regard for spiritual things. Jacob was sly and maybe a little bit of a "goody-goody," but he loved God and valued the things of the Spirit.

You probably remember the rest of the story. When it came time for Isaac to confer the blessing, Esau must have forgotten (or denied) the deal he made with Jacob. Now, God always has a way to accomplish His will, and He would have found a way to transfer Isaac's blessing from one brother to the other. He could have given Isaac a vision or used any number of ways to communicate His desire for Jacob to be given the blessing. Even though it was entirely unnecessary, Jacob and his mother plotted a way to deceive the dying Isaac.

Jacob and Rebecca thought they had to *help* God. Sound familiar? Do you recall that Abraham also tried to help God? This sin is familiar to many of us. Although the trick Jacob and Rebecca played ultimately resulted in God's will being fulfilled, the devious way they did it caused a serious detour in Jacob's life. After scamming his father and brother, Jacob had to run for his life. Jacob had a lot to learn before God could activate the stolen blessings. He had to be cheated by a deceiver greater than himself and literally wrestle with God to learn the lessons that would change his heart and allow him to return home and enjoy God's blessing.

God's Old Testament *"Favorites?"*

Flawed people who found grace and were greatly used by God in the Old Testament...

Noah got drunk
Moses stuttered
David was too small for his armor
Hosea's wife was a prostitute
Amos' only training was in fig tree pruning
Jacob was a liar and deceiver
Miriam was a gossip
Solomon was too rich
Abraham was too old
Naomi was a widow
Jonah ran away from God
David was a murderer and had an affair
Samson's hair was too long
Gideon was a doubter
Jeremiah was depressed and suicidal
Elijah was burned out

The Man Who Had It All— and Lost Everything

So far, we've traced God's blessing to Abraham, Isaac, and Jacob, but Jacob had 12 sons. Reuben was Jacob's first-born son and first in line for the blessings of priest, king, and the double-portion birthright. However, Reuben blew it and lost the blessing.

Jacob's 12 sons each fathered one of the tribes of Israel. Jacob's favorite and best-known son was Joseph (with the coat of many colors). Reuben had an affair with Jacob's concubine and played a part in selling his brother Joseph as a slave. Reuben could have repented and been forgiven, but he didn't; therefore, he lost his entire first-born blessing. Reuben should have gotten the priesthood, but instead it went to Levi; Reuben could have gotten the kingship, but it went to Judah; Reuben was supposed to received the double-portion, but that went to Joseph.

When the time came for Jacob to give blessings to the sons of Joseph, Jacob (the man who had deceived *his* father to obtain the blessing of the first born) did a *"cross*over" himself. First, he adopted Joseph's sons, Manasseh and Ephraim. When it came time to transfer God's double-portion blessing upon Joseph's seed, Jacob placed his right hand across to the youngest son, Ephraim, who was on his left, and placed his left hand across to the eldest, Manasseh, who was on his right. With his arms forming a *cross*, Jacob gave the greater blessing to the younger son.

Crossover Through Calvary

> ... *To Him who loved us and **washed us from our sins in His own blood, and has made us kings and priests** to His God and Father, to Him be glory and dominion forever and ever. Amen* (Revelation 1:5,6 NKJ).

The *crossover* for you and me came through the *Cross*. When Adam sinned, mankind and nature were cursed. We were cursed with sin, sickness, and failure—sinfulness became our nature, sickness our inclination, and failure our destiny.

> ...***Cursed is the ground for your sake;*** *in toil you shall eat of it all the days of your life.* ***Both thorns and thistles it shall bring forth for you,*** *and you shall eat the herb of the field.* ***In the sweat of your face you shall eat bread till you return to the ground,*** *for out of it you were taken; for dust you are, and to dust you shall return* (Genesis 3:17-19 NKJ).

Got Weakness? Get Grace!

Do you ever feel like you are battling to succeed against odds that are stacked against you? You are—your "ground is cursed." Does it seem that no matter how hard you try, whatever you do, you can't get ahead? Do your efforts seem to produce "thorns and thistles"? No matter how much you work, does it seem like things never improve? Yes, you and all mankind are cursed...but Jesus came to *cross*over your life from "cursed" to *blessed*.

Picture your *cross*over: You are standing before the judgment throne of God, and Jesus takes the Father's right hand of blessing and switches it from His head to *your* head, and takes the left hand of judgment from your forehead and moves it to His own! You have made the *cross*over from cursed to blessed.

> *Christ has redeemed us from the curse of the law, having become a curse for us (for it is written, "Cursed is everyone who hangs on a tree"), that the blessing of Abraham might come upon the Gentiles in Christ Jesus, that we might receive the promise of the Spirit through faith* (Galatians 3:13,14 NKJ).

Perhaps you are wondering, "If the curse has been removed from my life, why am I still doing sinful things, getting sick, and failing in life? The answer is that you haven't yet received God's grace for those things. I need to say this again so that you will really notice it: *If you are born-again but living under a curse, it's because you haven't received God's blessing through grace for your need.* Oh, you may have received the grace that provides salvation, but you haven't received God's grace to overcome the curse of sin as it is expressed in your life.

You need a "renaissance" in your thinking! Come out of the "dark ages" of religious tradition and into the light of the truth about God's grace. God loves *YOU*! He gave His Son to save *you* from sin *and its curse upon your life*. God didn't just pull you from "the pit" to leave you lying in the dirt. God is saying to you,

> ...*My grace is sufficient for you, for My strength is made perfect in* [your] *weakness...* (II Corinthians 12:9 NKJ).

Got any weaknesses? Get God's grace!

The *Good* Twin

If you are born-again, residing within you is a *younger* twin. The "you" you know was born in the *natural* and is made up of your body, mind, emotions, desires, and will. The "new you" was born in the *supernatural* when you received Jesus as Savior and Lord. Your new nature is the *younger* part of you. Just as He did in the Old Testament, God made a *cross*over and said, "the older will serve the younger" and gave the authority and blessing to the younger, so your *new* nature is to rule over your old. God is calling you to *live* out of your *new* nature rather than the old:

> ...*put off your old self, which is being corrupted by its deceitful desires; to be made new in the attitude of your minds; and to put on the new self, created to be like God in true righteousness and holiness* (Ephesians 4:22-24 NIV).

Not only is your new nature meant to dominate your flesh—your passions and inclinations—but it also has been empowered to rule over the curse of sin upon

God's New Testament *"Favorites"* ?

Flawed people who found grace and were used of God in the New Testament...

Timothy had ulcers
Thomas was a doubter
Peter feared a young girl's ridicule
Lazarus was dead
John was self-righteous
Paul was a murderer
Jesus was too poor
John the Baptist was a loudmouth
Martha was a worrywart
John Mark got homesick and quit
     his ministry
Peter and Paul had bad tempers

your life. Success, health, wealth, joy, and victory are in your new nature. Your new nature and new success in life come through the Cross—make the *cross*over and enjoy the benefits.

> *His divine power has given us everything we need for life and godliness through our knowledge of him who called us by his own glory and goodness. Through these he has given us his very great and precious promises, so that through them you may participate in the divine nature and escape the corruption in the world caused by evil desires* (II Peter 1:3,4 NIV).

Success, health, wealth, joy, and victory are in your new nature.

Let me illustrate this with a story. In my church, we have home cell groups. A person in one of the cell groups invited an acquaintance to attend, a man who did not attend our church or any other. He had a horrible past and among other terrible things, as a child, he had experienced sexual abuse. The first several weeks he attended the home meetings, the man sat with his head down, obviously depressed. He didn't remain for prayer or fellowship—just slipped in and out. The person who invited him kept in contact with him. Suddenly, the man seemed to change! His chin came off his chest and he became radiant! People noticed a nearly visible glow about him. Many people didn't even recognize him because he looked like an entirely different person. What happened? He made the *cross*over; he accepted Jesus into his life, and began to live in the *new* nature:

> *Therefore, if anyone is in Christ, he is a new creation; old things have passed away; behold, all things have become new* (II Corinthians 5:17 NKJ).

Long Lost Heir

> *But in these last days he has spoken to us by his* **Son, whom he appointed heir of all things,** *and through whom he made the universe* (Hebrews 1:2 NIV).

Jesus *is* the Son and heir to God's power and authority. It is vital that you know and believe that Jesus was not just a good man, a prophet, a great teacher, or a wise man, but that He is unquestionably the Son of the Living God. Jesus must be *the* Son for you to be a son and long lost heir of God.

The blood Jesus sacrificed upon the cross has bridged the chasm of sin that separated God and man. We have been adopted as sons, not because of our innate goodness or "the god within," as some would claim, but by means of our connection to Christ through His blood sacrifice.

> *The Spirit himself testifies with our spirit that we are God's children. Now if we are children,*

then we are heirs—heirs of God and co-heirs with Christ, if indeed we share in his sufferings in order that we may also share in his glory (Romans 8:16,17 NIV).

Yes, there is suffering when you follow Jesus. Most of the suffering is a result of denying the lusts and desires of the *old* nature, and imposing by force, when necessary, the *new* nature. However, that process becomes progressively less "painful" as the old nature learns that it no longer rules.

Sometimes you may be persecuted because you belong to Christ. Although most of us hate to acknowledge it, suffering *is* a fact of life. What we sometimes fail to remember is that even if you live for yourself in sin, you will suffer. The suffering for sin, however, is harsher and more painful, and sin's final reward is really ugly...death! Although suffering for Christ may not be pleasant, at least it brings a great reward—the benefits far outweigh the cost. Paul expressed it well when he said:

I consider that our present sufferings are not worth comparing with the glory that will be revealed in us (Romans 8:18 NIV).

"Ha, Ha Devil!"

Having disarmed principalities and powers, He made a public spectacle of them, triumphing over them in it (Colossians 2:15 NKJ).

The Bible says that we were created a little lower than the angels, and Satan, a fallen archangel, has even greater power and authority than angels do. Yet God's Word tells us that when Jesus died and descended to hell as a *man*, He beat Satan on his own turf. Jesus wrestled and bested Satan, taking from him the keys of his authority:

> *I am he that liveth, and was dead; and, behold, I am alive for evermore, Amen; and have the keys of hell and of death* (Revelation 1:18).

Don't you suppose Satan was embarrassed that Jesus, with only the power of a righteous man, bested him in front of his cohorts? We are heirs to the *same power* and authority over Satan. *You* can embarrass the devil, too! You can rebuke, bind, and forbid him as you stand upon God's Word and use the powerful name of Jesus.

Homeless Millionaire

Hebrews 1:2 says that Jesus is the *"...heir of all things,..."* and according to Romans 8:17, we are *"... joint-heirs with Christ...."* Being joint-heirs with the One Who is heir to all things, why do we limit our inheritance? We seriously restrict what we allow God to do in our behalf. Whether we think that grace is limited to salvation, it's "too good to be true," that we need to earn "merit" points, or that we are unworthy—the result is that we live far below our level of inheritance.

What if you were a poor and destitute street person, and your rich aunt died and left you $50,000,000 but you continued to sleep under bridges and beg for food? Then, when someone asked why you continued to live a deprived lifestyle, you answered, "I can't believe it's true. This must be a hoax because it has never happened to any of my penniless friends. I'm just a bum and don't deserve to have that kind of money. When I get myself cleaned up and become a useful person, I'll accept some of the money."

We have to *wake up* to what Jesus accomplished upon the cross! Though we are joint-heirs with Christ, many of us exist far below the spiritual "poverty line"—living *under* spiritual bridges and *begging* scraps of blessing. Grace says, "You don't have to deserve what I've given you. You just have to *believe* it and *receive* it by faith."

Touched by an Angel

Are not all angels ministering spirits sent to serve those who will inherit salvation? (Hebrews 1:14 NIV).

Some time ago I met with several pastors' wives from a large church in Indonesia. They were recounting their experience during the terrible religious riots that raged through their city. Many, many Christian churches were burned during the riots. (The country of Indonesia is primarily Muslim.)

Their church has an attendance of more than 6,000 people on Sundays. However, God had spoken to this church several years before and told them not to put up a sign with the name on the church. They thought that was a curious thing for God to say, but they were obedient.

Eventually, the riots spread to the neighborhood where this church is located, and the rioters asked the Muslim people of the neighborhood how to find the church. They were adamant. "We have a list of churches to burn and we know there is a church here by the name of 'Jesus is Lord.' Tell us where it is!" The neighborhood Muslims replied, "There is no church in our area. You must be thinking of the church over in the next neighborhood." When the rioters discovered the truth, the Muslims of the neighborhood formed a circle around the church to protect it, and the church wasn't destroyed.

Why did this church have such favor with the local Muslims? Because the Muslims set up food stands outside the church, and after service the Christians would buy their food. As the Muslims stood protecting the church, they shouted to rioters, "We need these Christians, don't you dare burn them down! We need their money." I believe that among the protectors in the crowd were others besides the Muslims—I think there were angels "all around" that church.

Miserable Existence or Exuberant LIVING?

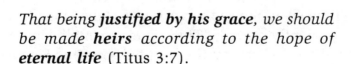

> *That being **justified by his grace**, we should be made **heirs** according to the hope of **eternal life** (Titus 3:7).*

When you were born, you received *bios* life, which means "physical life." You, like everyone who has gone before, will live for an appointed number of years; then your physical body will die. When you made the *cross*over through the Cross, however, you received *zoe* life. *Zoe* life is the best possible quality of life; it is "abundant life."

Recently, I was flying back to Denver from Orlando, Florida and was seated by a well-dressed, successful-looking man. After he watched the movie, we visited a little. I had my Bible on my lap and he recognized me from television. He told me that he grew up in a small Oklahoma town, but had become very successful and now had homes in Singapore, Canada, and other places in the world. He told me that his job required him to travel a great deal. As he reminisced about his childhood he said, "When I was growing up in that little Oklahoma town, I went to a Baptist church and I had a Sunday School teacher who really made us memorize scripture. We memorized not just verses but whole epistles." Wistfully, he added, "Those were wonderful times."

Then he told me that he had attended a university and heard things contrary to God's Word. Before long the wisdom of man replaced God's wisdom in his system of beliefs. A note of sadness crept into his voice as he sighed, "I still believe Jesus is the Son of God, but I just don't have what I had in those years before my thinking turned." Do you see what occurred? The older nature had begun to rule over the younger and the *zoe* life he had known was replaced with *bios* living— he had gained wealth and success but lost the "abundant life."

I silently prayed, "This man is so intelligent, please God don't let me say anything stupid. Give me *Your* words for this man." I said, "Could I ask you, do you have peace in your heart? Are you *really* happy? Do you feel *good* about yourself?"

> # Living in the new nature, *zoe* life, is *real* living.

He replied, "No, I don't have peace. Though I'm very successful, I am *very* unhappy."

So I asked, "Where do you think your *true* source of happiness is?

He smiled and said, "I know what you're going to say."

"What are *you* going to say?"

"It's Jesus. But, I can't go to church. I travel all the time."

"Do you have a Bible?

"Yes, but I never read it or carry it with me anymore."

"Would you start carrying your Bible?"

"I can do that."

"Would you read the gospel of John?"

"Yes," he replied.

When we got off the plane, he handed me his card and said, "Here's my e-mail address. Would you pray for me?" It was *already* beginning to happen: he was getting out of the "old" man and returning to the "new." Living in the new nature, *zoe* life, is *real* living.

If this true account has reminded you of a better time in *your* life, it's *not* too late. Those "better days" don't belong to past *times,* they belong to a past *relationship,* and it can be yours again. Although you can't go back in time, you can go back spiritually and reconnect with God—turn from the "old" man to the "new" and rediscover *zoe* life.

You, Yes You! Are a King

The new you has *authority*. Remember, you are a joint-heir with Jesus, so think about the things He took authority over when He walked the earth. I am going to remind you of a few of them.

- **Reign Over Demons**

Jesus had *authority over demons,* and so do you.

> *The people were all so amazed that they asked each other, "What is this? A new teaching—and with authority! He [Jesus] even gives orders to evil spirits and they obey him"* (Mark 1:27 NIV).

You may recall that when Jesus sent out his disciples to minister on their own, they cast out demons in the name of Jesus. So can you!

- **Rule Over Weather**

Jesus had authority over the weather. Perhaps you remember the time Jesus was sleeping on a ship, when a storm arose so fierce that the disciples feared for their lives. They woke Jesus, who stilled the storm. Afterwards, they asked:

> *"...What kind of man is this? Even the winds and the waves obey him!" (Matthew 8:27 NIV).*

The week prior to my second crusade in Pakistan,

the Islamabad area experienced some of the hardest rains and worst flash-flooding in history. In the area where my meetings were to be held, hundreds of lives were lost. When my event coordinator arrived a week before the outdoor services were to start, the meeting grounds were still extremely muddy. He encouraged the Pakistani Christians there to begin to pray for the weather. At home, we also prayed. The rains stopped! By the time I arrived with the ministry team, the grounds were dry.

We continued to pray for the weather, and every night of the weeklong meeting, we heard distant thunder during the services—but rain never once interrupted us! One evening, the minute the meeting was over, it started to pour, and it rained long and hard that night. In fact, it rained so hard that it knocked down the tent we were using for the daytime pastors' seminars. In spite of that, we only missed one training session. Then the sun came out and dried the meeting grounds, and we were able to have services that evening.

• **Power Over Sickness**
Jesus had authority over sickness. Countless times Jesus healed the sick, and so can you. Taking authority over sickness is the right of every believer.

Jesus healed the sick and so did His disciples:

And they cast out many devils, and anointed with oil many that were sick, and healed them (Mark 6:13).

Believers have the promise that God will use them in healing the sick. When Jesus was preparing the disciples for His death and departure from their lives, He surprised them by exclaiming:

> *I tell you the truth, anyone who has **faith in me** will do what I have been doing. He will do even greater things than these, because I am going to the Father. And **I will do whatever you ask in my name**, so that the Son may bring glory to the Father. You may **ask me for anything in my name, and I will do it** (John 14:12-14 NIV).*

So Jesus was saying that we too can heal the sick, but our power to heal is based upon *faith* in Him and use of His name. However, did you notice the prerequisite to this promised power: *"because I am going to the Father"*? Jesus knew that He would soon die upon a cross, and that the cross would make possible our *"cross*over" to be sons and heirs of His authority over disease.

Anemic Ambassador or Powerful Priest?

> *Therefore, since we have a great high priest who has gone through the heavens, Jesus the Son of God, let us hold firmly to the faith we profess* (Hebrews 4:14 NIV).

When Jesus walked the earth, He was not a priest. You probably remember that Israel's priests were all descendants of Levi, one of the 12 sons of Jacob. They were priests of the Old Covenant. Jesus was a descendant of David, who was of the tribe of Judah and not qualified to be a priest. Yet after His death, Jesus became the High Priest of the *New* Covenant between God and man. The book of Hebrews describes the dramatic scene of Jesus entering the Holy of Holies of God's temple in heaven and assuming the role of High Priest. He did not offer the blood of an animal to *cover up* sin, but presented His own sinless blood to *take away* the sins of mankind.

Once Jesus had secured our salvation, He sat down next to God at the highest place of honor. Hebrews 8:1 says:

> ...*We do have such a high priest, who sat down*
> *at the right hand of the throne of the Majesty*
> *in heaven,...* (NIV).

The "right hand" always has to do with *power*. Jesus is not one of *many* sons of God. He doesn't share a place of honor with Buddha, Allah, or Satan. Jesus is not some minor power in charge of sweeping up stardust, He

> ...*is at God's right hand—with angels,*
> *authorities and powers in submission to him*
> (I Peter 3:22 NIV).

Priests have power with God and the Bible says (see Revelation 1:6) that you are a priest. You have not only the authority of a king, but the power of a priest to bring to bear upon the circumstances of your life and the lives of others. You are an *heir of Christ's authority* and a joint-heir to the power and authority of God. If you are a victim of man or Satan, you don't have to be. The *only* way they could crucify Jesus was with His consent, but

Jesus paid the price so that you could go free. Start acting like a priest and a king by using your God-given authority!

Take a Break

> *Come to me, all you who are weary and burdened, and I will give you rest....and you will find rest for your souls. For my yoke is easy and my burden is light* (Matthew 11:28-30 NIV).

There is a very famous photograph of a farmer and his wife taken during the Great Depression. The farmer has a horse's harness around his neck and his wife, her hands on the plow, trudges against high winds through dusty fields as, together, they *push* and *pull* against seemly impossible odds, to make furrows for planting an uncertain harvest.

These poor, brave souls were determined to plant a crop even though their horse was dead or had been sold to pay expenses. There may be times when you feel like that farmer and his wife—bone tired, hopeless, barely existing from one day to the next—dragging an impossibly heavy weight.

The weights that pull us down are often not physical ones but spiritual, mental and emotional burdens—sin, worry, anxiety, fear, anger, and the like. *You don't have to live that way!* Jesus, if you will allow Him, will remove your burden and replace it with His yoke where you can find "rest for your soul."

Many Christians need to enter into the "rest" spoken of in Hebrews 4:9,10:

There remains, then, a Sabbath-rest for the people of God; for anyone who enters God's rest also rests from his own work, just as God did from his (NIV).

They need to "rest from their *own* work" and begin to believe God for the supernatural in their situations. I'm not saying that you should be lazy or sloppy concerning the issues of your life. I am saying, when the time comes that you have *done all* you know to do, stop your "doing" and start "standing" in faith upon God's Word for your situations. God has His hands out to you, reaching for your burden. Give it up! Give the *care* of your situations to God—trust in His grace, His Word, and the power of your faith.

Rescued From the Briar Patch

Everyone has thorns in their life, things that painfully prick them. Some thorns are just mild annoyances, but others are long, painful, and can pierce to the heart. The good news is that Jesus has taken our thorns and made them into a crown of glory!

Before Jesus was crucified, when the Roman soldiers beat and mocked Him, they placed upon His head a *crown* of thorns. Thorns pierced His head. Jesus suffered this excruciating pain so that you and I could live free of the thorns of life. When you offer up to Him your thorns of failure, loss, and regret, Jesus substitutes a crown of life.

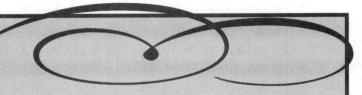

THE LORD'S SUPPER

The ritualistic practice, usually during a worship service, in which Christians partake of bread and wine (or grape juice) with the purpose of remembering Christ, receiving strength from Him, and rededicating themselves to His cause. It is one of two sacraments or ordinances instituted by Christ to be observed by His church until He returns.

(Reprinted by permission from Nelson's Illustrated Bible Dictionary © 1986, Thomas Nelson Publishers)

"...Be faithful, even to the point of death, and I will give you the crown of life" (Revelation 2:10 NIV).

This Is It!

Perhaps you are thinking: "Marilyn, that sounds good, real good. I've done everything I know to do, but I just can't seem to live this 'better way,' in the 'new' nature. I don't have the 'abundant life.'"

In order to make the *cross*over, the first thing you must do is come to terms with the fact that you, your talents, IQ, and qualities are not enough to propel you into the "abundant life." You can't perfect yourself enough. You can't read enough self-help books to achieve it. You can't earn it by your good deeds and righteous acts, or gain it by osmosis. The only hope you–and everyone else– have of living a life of complete victory is to go outside yourself, find the divine power, and make it a part of you. To make the *cross*over, to live in the zoe life, you must learn to become a "partaker."

"Eat My Flesh"

You must *partake,* become one with the sacrifice that has made possible your *cross*over. In the Old Testament, after making a sacrifice for someone, the priests would eat the parts of the lamb or other animal that was sacrificed. In doing this, they became one with the altar: *"...are not they which eat of the sacrifices partakers of the altar?"* (I Corinthians 10:18).

In the sacrament of communion, a believer eats the "bread" and drinks the "wine" or grape juice, which symbolizes *partaking* of Christ, *your* sacrifice. Jesus himself underscored the importance of *partaking* when he said...

> ...*I tell you the truth, unless you eat the flesh of the Son of Man and drink his blood, you have no life in you. Whoever eats my flesh and drinks my blood has eternal life, ...Whoever eats my flesh and drinks my blood remains in me, and I in him. Just as the living Father sent me and I live because of the Father, so the **one who feeds on me will live because of me*** (John 6:53-57 NIV).

Jesus was not suggesting cannibalism, although many of the people listening that day thought that was His meaning and were offended. No, Jesus was telling them that *He* was going to be their sin sacrifice. He added that in order for them to receive the benefit of it, they must internalize or *partake* of it.

Cultivating the New You

What does all this mean to you? It means that Jesus' sacrifice for *your* sins and the curse upon your life is merely a *potential* benefit until you take it for your own. You are just an *observer,* not a partaker in the *crossover,* until you personally say to God in all honesty, "I recognize that I am a sinner. Please cleanse me of my sins. Jesus, come into my heart and make me a new person."

However, when you ask God for forgiveness, He gives you much more—He gives you a "new" nature. The "new" you is like a baby in some ways. It needs attention, love, food, and friends. For you to live out of the "new" you and not the "old" nature, your new nature also needs to mature and grow strong. It does so when you *continue to* partake of Jesus.

Partake can mean "fellowship." You continue partaking of Jesus by associating yourself with a church. If you are not participating in a church, or if you are unhappy where you attend, ask God to lead you to the right place. God has a specific church for you to participate in and a special pastor to be your shepherd. To flourish, the "new you" needs the fellowship of other believers which can be found in a home-cell group, and you need the leadership of a pastor who will speak the words of God into your life.

Munch the Message

The more you *know* Him, the more *power* you receive.

For you to live the "abundant life," you need to establish a *friendship* with God. He loves you, and when you are born-again, you love Him, but a friendship or relationship is built on more than love—it's built on communication.

Remember when you first met that "special someone"? You didn't just smile at each other across a crowded room. You got together and talked, and from those conversations came understanding of each other. It's really as simple as that. You need to talk to Him and He needs to talk to you, too. You need to learn His ways because those are the "ways" to real living. The more you *know* Him, the more power you receive:

> *His divine power has **given us everything we need for life and godliness through our knowledge of him** who called us by his own glory and goodness* (II Peter 1:3 NIV).

The best way to partake of and come to know God is through the fellowship of His Word. Eat (read) and chew (meditate) on the Word of God. You need to internalize it so that His words live in you:

> *If you abide in Me, and My words abide in you, you will ask what you desire, and it shall be done for you* (John 15:7 NKJ).

Will You Dare to Believe?

God is looking for people who will think BIG—people like Abraham who will really believe what He says. He wants people who will look beyond themselves and their own meager abilities, beyond defeating doctrines, beyond the merit system, beyond circumstances, trials, and tribulations and *believe* Him when He says:

> And **I will do whatever you ask** *in my name,*
> *so that the Son may bring glory to the Father.*
> *You may* **ask me for anything in my name,**
> **and I will do it** *(John 14:13,14 NIV).*

Can you dare to believe it's true?...

> *He who did not spare his own Son, but gave*
> *him up for us all—how will he not also, along*
> *with him, graciously* **give us all things?**
> (Romans 8:32 NIV).

"Everything" and "all things" are big concepts. They challenge your capacity to believe.

I've never counted them myself, but I'm told there are 7,000 promises in God's Word. Regardless of their number, I know that God has a promise for every situation that you will ever face. To live in your "new" or "divine" nature, you need to become a partaker in God's promises:

> *Through these* **he has given us his**
> **very great and precious promises, so**
> **that through them you may participate in**
> **the divine nature** *and escape the corruption in*
> *the world caused by evil desires*(II Peter 1:4 NIV).

Me Too?

One of the Greek words translated "partaker" is *sugkoinonos*, which means to "partake jointly." In a letter Paul wrote while in jail, he says to the church at Philippi:

> *...whether I am in chains or defending and confirming the gospel, all of you share in God's grace with me* (Philippians 1:7 NIV).

Paul is saying that we share or partake in one another's grace. When Paul received grace in prison, they received grace in Philippi. When a wonderful thing happens to someone else, know that it affects you, too. When you see a healing or breakthrough in someone's family, job, finances, etc., remind yourself that God really does answer prayer. Use their victory to empower your faith for the same blessing.

We also share or partake in what was promised in the Old Testament to Abraham and the Jews:

> *...that the blessing of Abraham might come upon the Gentiles in Christ Jesus, that we might receive the promise of the Spirit through faith.* (Galatians 3:14 NKJ).

Help Wanted

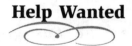

No divinity school training? No seminary degree? You can't sing or speak in public? *No* special talents or abilities of *any* kind? No sweat! God's "help wanted" ad reads: "No education, experience, or resume required. Just come and bring a willing heart."

> *Therefore, holy brethren, **partakers of the heavenly calling**, consider the Apostle and High Priest of our confession, Christ Jesus,...* (Hebrews 3:1 NKJ).

What is your calling? God wants you to understand what you are called, anointed, and equipped to do in the Body of Christ. When Paul explained about your "heavenly calling" and the connection between believers, he likened it to a human body. Think about your physical body. Every part has a specific job to do. If, for example, you were to lose the use of an arm, the rest of the body would suffer because it would have to work harder to make up for the loss. If you are not active in a church or ministry, then everyone is the loser! You need to discover your "heavenly calling" and get to work. We *need* you and you need us!

When Moses was born, his parents recognized that he was a child of destiny. They knew he was not meant to be a slave like them. That is why Moses' mother put him in a basket and sailed him down to the part of the river that served as a bathtub for a princess of Egypt. Moses had a heavenly calling upon his life, and so do you.

> **No education, experience, or resume required. Just come and bring a willing heart.**

Many believe that an ambitious Egyptian princess adopted Moses, then raised and trained him to be the next Pharaoh. Moses, however, did not forget his roots. When he saw an Egyptian slave master beating a Hebrew slave, he became enraged and killed the Egyptian. After that, Moses was a hunted man. He fled Egypt and ended up tending someone else's sheep on the backside of the desert. Moses made a serious mistake and consequently almost missed his calling.

Moses was called, equipped, trained, and anointed to bring the Israelites out of Egyptian bondage. However, God could have used another person to do it, and would have, if necessary. Moses needed that job more than God needed him to do it. Moses would never have been really happy or fulfilled in life doing anything else. Do you think a man raised to shepherd a nation could be happy herding sheep on the backside of nowhere? Like a peg hand-carved to fit a special hole, Moses was God's perfect choice to be the liberator of Israel.

God has handcrafted *you* for a special "heavenly calling." Possibly, unknown to you, He is in the process of equipping, anointing, and training you to do something very special for His kingdom. If you don't know what it is, find out and begin doing it, even in a small way. You will never find *real* happiness, until you do.

Survival Training

*...My son, do not make light of the Lord's discipline, and do not lose heart when he rebukes you, because **the Lord disciplines those he loves**, and he punishes everyone he accepts as a son. Endure hardship as discipline; God is treating you as sons. For what son is not disciplined by his father? If you are not disciplined (and everyone undergoes discipline), then you are illegitimate children and not true sons* (Hebrews 12:5-8 NIV).

Children are not born with the knowledge they need to "make it" in life. Unlike many animals that are born with natural instincts for survival, without instruction children will be failures. Christians are the same—we also need training. This is the element of *partaking* most of us would rather skip. I'm not going to sugarcoat it—learning how to live in your "new" nature is difficult at times. I'm sure that when you were young, you never liked discipline from your parents, but now you appreciate it and see that it was necessary. The same is true of God's training.

Discipline is bitter but the rewards are sweet! Each lesson teaches you how to gain more of your inheritance. Each instruction makes you better, happier, and more successful. During the most difficult times of training, God's love and grace are with you. Unlike earthly parents, God never disciplines you because he is angry with you. He never "puts you down" to make you feel bad. God never manipulates you or puts you on a "guilt trip." God's discipline is *always* for your good and never for His personal satisfaction. It is proof positive of your acceptance into the family of God:

> *No discipline seems pleasant at the time, but painful. Later on, however, it produces a harvest of righteousness and peace for those who have been trained by it* (Hebrews 12: 11 NIV).

Weakness is Perfect

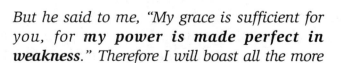

> *But he said to me, "My grace is sufficient for you, for **my power is made perfect in weakness**." Therefore I will boast all the more*

gladly about my weaknesses, so that Christ's
power may rest on me (II Corinthians 12:9 NIV).

"The weaker I am the better!" Can you believe that
the man who evangelized most of his world and wrote much
of the New Testament would make such a statement? The
Apostle Paul was a man of incredible talent, zeal, and
education. Like Moses, he had all the tools to do a
phenomenal job for God, yet he discovered a way to be
even better and more successful. Paul discovered that
weakness is the secret to power.

Perhaps you're thinking, "If weakness is the key to
success, I'm bound to be successful. I've got plenty of
weaknesses." Actually, the key is recognizing that even your
most talented performance is merely "human effort" and
will produce only *natural* results. To get *supernatural* results,
you must *admit* that your best is weak compared to God's
smallest effort.

Most of us don't look to God for help until we feel
overwhelmed, until we come up against something we
can't overcome on our own. Consequently, we call upon
God at the last possible moment, hoping that He will give
us the best possible miracle. If we would go to God at the
onset of a problem, many times with God's help and
wisdom, it could be solved quickly and easily.

Until we realize that we will have better success if
we do things in *God's* power, we obstruct the work of God's
grace in our life. The "abundant life" requires the
supernatural. Only as we rely upon the infusion of the *zoe*
life of God can we live supernaturally. Paul explained this
zoe life to the people of Athens by saying, "*...for in Him we
live and move and have our being,...*" (Acts 17:28 NKJ).

Face the Furnace

God can answer your prayers concerning your situations in one of two ways: He can immediately deliver you or He can enter the situation with you, fortify you to withstand it, and bring you out a winner. When Babylon held Israel captive, the three Hebrew children were required to bow to an idol, and they refused. As punishment, they were to be thrown into a furnace and burned to death. While Shadrach, Meshach, and Abednego awaited their execution, I think it is safe to say that they prayed to God for deliverance.

Did God cause an earthquake, break open their jail, and have angels whisk them to safety? No, He did not deliver them *outside* their problem so they wouldn't have to face the furnace. Rather, He delivered them by accompanying them *inside* their problem and supernaturally seeing them through.

No one wants to "face the furnace." However, it is often God's best solution for your situation. So when the IRS asks you to drop by for a chat, remember that God may not make this problem disappear in a puff of smoke. However, He does have some used-but-serviceable asbestos suits you can borrow, and He can fit your appointment into His busy schedule!

At those times, you can give your fears to God, lean back with total trust into His embrace and say, "My *only* hope is You, Lord! I give my life into Your care because I know that You love me and that Your power is *perfected* in my weakness."

I dare you to try it! Totally trust God for a situation beyond your control and refuse to worry about it. When you totally entrust your problem to God, you will discover that you need never again live in fear and anxiety. Then you will be able to say with the writer of Hebrews, *"...The Lord is my helper, I will not fear. What can man do to me?"* (Hebrews 13:6 NKJ).

Holler at Your Mountain

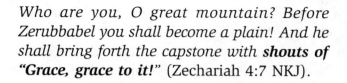

*Who are you, O great mountain? Before Zerubbabel you shall become a plain! And he shall bring forth the capstone with **shouts of "Grace, grace to it!"*** (Zechariah 4:7 NKJ).

Who doesn't have a mountain? A mountain can be anything that towers over you and looks big, scary, imposing, or impossible. If you are facing a mountain and it seems to be growing and getting ready to topple on you...you can shout your mountain down! But, you have to say the *right* thing.

Instead of speaking to our mountain, too often, we whine about it. We say things like...

"I'm from a dysfunctional family."

"I've had this problem since I was...."

"I just never got a good education so I can't...."

"I have this physical or mental handicap that keeps me from...."

"My pastor/wife/husband/children let me down."

God never told us to speak *about* the mountain. Instead, He says we are to declare *to* our mountain, *"Who* do you think *you* are to try and stand against a child of the Most High God! You better get ready—get ready because God's grace is going to smash you flat!"

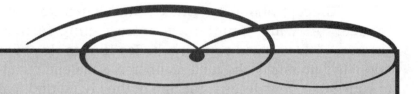

CAPSTONE

The uppermost stone in a building project, sometimes used to tie two intersecting walls together [*"Who are you O great mountain? Before Zerubbabel you shall become a plain! And he shall bring forth the capstone with shouts of 'Grace, grace to it!'"*] (Zechariah 4:7 NKJ).
 As the top stone of a structure or wall, the capstone was the crowning point.

(Reprinted by permission from *Nelson's Illustrated Bible Dictionary* © 1986, Thomas Nelson Publishers)

"Grace!" Shout it: "Grace!" and when you shout "Grace!" at your mountain you are calling forth the "capstone"—Jesus—in your behalf. See Him as He appears *now*, He's no longer the mild-mannered Nazarene pictured in your Bible. Your Jesus is the Son of the Living God, more than a match for any mountain:

> *His head and hair were white like wool, as white as snow, and his eyes were like blazing fire. His feet were like bronze glowing in a furnace, and his voice was like the sound of rushing waters* (Revelation 1:14,15 NIV).

When you cry "Grace!" you've set a mighty champion up against your mole-hole of a mountain and it will *have to* fall.

Nonstop Grace

"You are going to live and not die!" the bleeding pastor's wife shouted through her tears as she cradled the bullet-riddled body of her dying husband.

He had been shot seven times and she had received a flesh wound. This pastor of a large church in Colombia had taken a stand against the drug cartel and assassination was the cartel's answer.

As he lay in her arms rapidly bleeding to death, she prayed and spoke life to his body. She cried out to God for grace for her dying husband. By God's grace, he lived and was brought to the United States for safety, treatment, and recuperation. Six months later this pastor and his wife boarded an airplane to return to Colombia. Don't you think this would have been a good time to retire? To stay in the U.S. and perhaps work with another ministry? These are people with the same fears and desires as you and me. Where did they get the courage to return to Colombia? They obtained their courage by claiming *more* grace.

Today, they have more than 1,500 small groups meeting in homes of their church congregation. Not long ago, they hosted a worldwide convention for cell group leaders and more than 200,000 people traveled to a nation torn by drug wars to learn from a modern-day Christian hero. This pastor and his wife received more grace, and so can you. God has *more* grace than you will *ever* need:

> *...how much more will those who receive **God's abundant provision of grace** and of the gift of righteousness reign in life through the one man, Jesus Christ* (Romans 5:17 NIV).

Unclaimed Inheritance

Although this book is coming to a close, I believe this is only the beginning for you. The utterly dependable and unfailing Word of God has opened your eyes to God's grace—grace that is especially reserved for you and your needs. Yes, as a son or daughter of God, you have an inheritance from Jesus through grace. However, an inheritance is only a *potential* blessing until the person who made the will dies. Jesus died for our sins more than 2,000 years ago and made possible the *cross*over to sonship. If you want to benefit from your inheritance, you must take the last step—*receive* it.

Warehoused in heaven are pallets stacked high with blessings that have your name stenciled on them. However, they will remain *unclaimed* unless you accept them through *grace*.

Do You Remember?

Do you remember why you picked up this book? Was it because you were looking for a way, *any way*, to make a "comeback" in your life? I want to remind you there *really* is a God and He *really* cares about your situation and He *really* has a comeback for you.

Don't dismiss these principles as "religious." They have nothing to do with "church" or the supposed "spiritual" things that you may know. This book is about *relationship*, a *real* relationship with a *real* God that really loves you in spite of who you are, where you have been, or what you have done. The question you face is this: will you miss the "deal" of your lifetime by walking away as the same person who picked up this book?

> **There really is a God and He really has a "comeback" for you.**

Do you remember the rich young man we talked about earlier who came to Jesus asking what he could do to gain eternal life? He was a good and moral man, but in the end he walked away. He missed out not only on eternal life, but also on an opportunity that only 12 people out of the billions who have walked this planet have had—to be a disciple of Christ! How could he have made such a stupid mistake? Easy! You and I make the same mistake every day. We believe that God evaluates our *worthiness* by the "merit system" before He gives us His grace.

Are you a person who, in your heart, believes that you're a hopeless "victim" of some disabling personal tragedy? If so, I want to encourage you to come out of your comfortable prison, your excuse for not "making it in life," and declare that by the grace of God your are *not* a victim but a VICTOR! Remember all those things you dreamed of doing and being? By God's grace, you *can* have a successful, happy, and meaningful life—it's not too late. Don't miss what could be your last opportunity for escape!

Are you a skeptic? Do you have a dogmatic doctrine that doesn't allow for a "do-gooder" God? Maybe your God is dark and angry, a hater of sinners, a vengeful person who loves only those who are "worthy" and punishes others at the slightest provocation. Ask yourself if your God could have sent "His only begotten Son" to die for the hideous sins of disgusting people who despised Him. Could it be that in the pages of this book you've caught a glimpse of a God whom you prefer to worship? God *really is* the kind and fair loving Father you always wanted but may never have had.

Spiritual Amnesia

The Bible says in John 8:32, *"And ye shall know the truth, and the truth shall make you free."* This is God's promise to you no matter who you are or where you're coming from—the truth about grace *will* set you free...if...and *only* if you take it inside you and begin to act upon it. If you don't grasp it, it will slip through your fingers like water and be gone. You really can't wait to decide–*this is your defining moment!*

I'm sorry to tell you that if you don't receive this truth *now*, the Bible says that you will suffer a memory loss. Perhaps you recall the parable Jesus gave to His disciples that compared the "truth" to a seed. He said:

> *When anyone hears the message about the kingdom and does not understand it, the evil one comes and snatches away what was sown in his heart. This is the seed sown along the path. The one who received the seed that fell on rocky places is the man who hears the word and at once receives it with joy. But since he has no root, he lasts only a short time. When trouble or persecution comes because of the word, he quickly falls away. The one who received the seed that fell among the thorns is the man who hears the word, but the worries of this life and the deceitfulness of wealth choke it, making it unfruitful. But the one who received the seed that fell on good soil is the man who hears the word and understands it. He produces a crop, yielding a hundred, sixty or thirty times what was sown* (Matthew 13:19-23 NIV).

The enemy doesn't *want* you to know that you have the *authority* of a king, the *power* of a priest, and a double-portion *blessing*—the assurance that every promise in the Bible belongs to you. He wants to steal this truth from you so that you will continue as you are. What will you do with this "seed"? Will you be the "good ground" and get a crop of grace, or is it possible that you won't even *remember* it tomorrow?

If I could look you in the eye and speak to you face-to-face, I would plead with you *"take the opportunity for grace. Seize the moment–take delivery of God's grace for your situation...He won't let you down."*

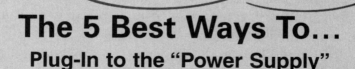

The 5 Best Ways To...
Plug-In to the "Power Supply"

1. Read the story of Abraham's obedience to God in offering Isaac as a sacrifice in Genesis 22:1-18. Then pray and ask God what He would have you offer Him upon an altar of obedience.

2. Make a list of the weaknesses, personal problems, and disabilities that are holding you back from being all that God wants you to be, then read and meditate on II Corinthians 12:9,10.

3. If things of your "old" nature, *bios* life, are crowding out the *zoe* life, your new nature, read Romans 6:3-14 and begin to "reckon" or consider yourself divorced through death from your sins and weaknesses.

4. Make a list of the areas of your life that seem to be "cursed." Then read and personalize Galatians 3:13, by inserting "me" and the name of your curse into the verse. For example: "Christ has redeemed [me] from the curse of [sickness], having become a curse for [me]..." (NKJ).

5. As a born-again person are you living in your God-given (kingship) authority over Satan and sickness? If not, write John 14:12-14 on an index card, put it in your pocket or purse, or over the sun-visor in your car, and read it every time you feel weak and incapable of dealing with life's situations.

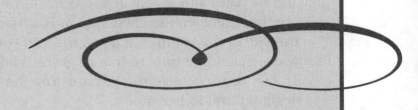

AfterWORD
Now What?

Grace is your stepladder to a wonderful life, and your first step is to receive salvation *through* grace. You truly can bounce back from any setback *when* you belong to the family of God. If you don't have a close relationship with God or you are unsure of your relationship with Him, isn't it time to take that *first* step?

Perhaps you *have* known God but made some bad choices and walked away from Him. Maybe you have run away from God to do your *own* "thing." He is standing with open arms in the middle of your highway home—waiting, waiting for your return. You will never *truly* know victory, *really* find peace, or experience how "good" life can be until you make peace with God and live by His grace. You can make things right with Him by a simple prayer.

Say it aloud or in your heart, but mean it:

Dear God, I come you as a sinner asking forgiveness for all my sins. I relinquish sin and its ways and accept Jesus as *the* Lord of my life. I receive the cleansing of His blood from *all* of sin's pollution. Steer me into Your ways. Teach me how to live in grace. Make of me the *exceptional* person You have designed me to be. Amen.

If you have prayed this prayer and meant it, find the coupon in the back pages of this book, fill it out, and mail it to me. I would like to send you free information to help you with your "new" life.

Get connected to God, pursue Him—read His Word, talk to Him daily in prayer, and find a church that will nurture you spiritually and help you to find your place in the Body of Christ.

Bibliography

Clarke, Adam. *Clarke's Commentary.* Seattle, Washington: Biblesoft, 1996.

Henry, Matthew. *Matthew Henry's Commentary On the Whole Bible: New Modern Edition electronic database.* Hendrickson Publishers, Inc., 1991.

Hickey, Marilyn. *Bible Encounter.* Denver, Colorado: Marilyn Hickey Ministries, 1987.

Hickey, Marilyn. *The Book of Job.* Denver, Colorado: Marilyn Hickey Ministries, 1990.

Lockyer, Sr., Herbert, ed. *Nelson's Illustrated Bible Dictionary.* Nashville, Tennessee: Thomas Nelson Publishers, 1986.

Vine, W.E. *Vine's Expository Dictionary of Biblical Words.* Nashville, Tennessee: Thomas Nelson Publishers, 1985.

Receive Jesus Christ as Lord and Savior of Your Life.

The Bible says, *"That if thou shalt confess with thy mouth the Lord Jesus, and shalt believe in thine heart that God raised him from the dead, thou shalt be saved. For with the heart man believeth unto righteousness; and with the mouth confession is made unto salvation"* (Romans 10:9,10).

To receive Jesus Christ as Lord and Savior of your life, sincerely pray this prayer from your heart:

Dear Jesus,

I believe that You died for me and that You rose again on the third day. I confess to You that I am a sinner and that I need Your love and forgiveness. Come into my life, forgive my sins, and give me eternal life. I confess You now as my Lord. Thank You for my salvation!

Signed _____ Date _____

Name   Mr. & Mrs.   Please print.
       Mr.
       Miss
       Mrs. _____

Address _____

City _____ State _____ Zip _____

Phone(H)(   ) _____

Write to us.
We will send you information to help you
with your new life in Christ.

Marilyn Hickey Ministries
P.O. Box 17340 • Denver, CO 80217 • 303-770-0400
www.mhmin.org

BOOKS BY MARILYN HICKEY

A Cry for Miracles $7.95
Acts of the Holy Spirit $7.95
Angels All Around $7.95
Armageddon $4.95
Ask Marilyn $9.95
Be Healed $9.95
Bible Encounter Classic Edition $24.95
Book of Revelation Comic Book (The) $3.00
Break the Generation Curse $7.95
Break the Generation Curse—Part 2 .... $9.95
Building Blocks for Better Families $4.95
Daily Devotional $7.95
Dear Marilyn $7.95
Devils, Demons, and Deliverance $9.95
Divorce Is Not the Answer $7.95
Freedom From Bondages $7.95
God's Covenant for Your Family $7.95
God's Rx for a Hurting Heart $4.95
How to Be a Mature Christian $7.95
Know Your Ministry $4.95
Maximize Your Day . . . God's Way $7.95
Miracle Signs and Wonders $24.95
Names of God (The) $7.95
Nehemiah—Rebuilding the Broken Places in Your Life $7.95
No. 1 Key to Success—Meditation (The) $4.95
Proverbs Classic Library Edition $24.95
Release the Power of the Blood Covenant $4.95
Satan-Proof Your Home $7.95
Signs in the Heavens $7.95
What Every Person Wants to Know About Prayer $4.95
When Only a Miracle Will Do $4.95
Your Miracle Source $4.95
Your Total Health Handbook—Body • Soul • Spirit $9.95

Prices are in U.S. dollars. If ordering in foreign currency, please calculate the current exchange rate.
www.mhmin.org

Visit
Marilyn
Hickey Ministries'

Website

www.mhmin.org